Just when I imagined I had God in a tidy box—as almighty, holy, sovereign, majestic and so forth—along comes Dylan DeMarsico to remind me that words like happy and laughter and dance also characterize our trinitarian God, grounding his argument in a careful reading of Scripture. My God-box has been blown open!

— **Mark Galli**, editor-in-chief of Christianity Today

Dylan's book *The Happy Trinity* has incredible insights into God's nature that will help Christians understand who He really is. I caught myself laughing and learning while turning its pages. In a healthy handling of Scriptures, Dylan brings clarity to us regarding God's wrath and the ever so needed knowledge of God's joy-unspeakable. Who would have thought that playfulness is a core part of our Lord's nature and the missing link in our theology?

— **Eric Perales**, Worship & Youth Pastor of Harvest Valley Church

I believe heaven is celebrating over the release of *The Happy Trinity*! The Scriptures tells us that God is zealous for His name. In other words, our Creator cares deeply about how the world sees and understands His nature and identity. This isn't because He's egotistical or insecure, but because the true knowledge of God is what will lead the nations into wholeness. This book provides a revolutionary window into the heart of God, helping to uncover the true "name" of our precious and joyful God!

— **Nicholas Padovani**, Senior Pastor of The Almond Branch, Author of *The Song of the Ages* series

THE HAPPY TRINITY

DYLAN DEMARSICO

Copyright © 2019 by Dylan DeMarsico

The Happy Trinity

by Dylan DeMarsico

Printed in the United States of America

ISBN-13: 978-0-9991806-2-4 (paperback)

ISBN-13: 978-0-9991806-3-1 (e-book)

All rights reserved solely by the author. The author guarantees all contents are original and do not infringe upon the legal rights of any other person or work. No part of this book may be reproduced in any form without the permission of the author.

Unless otherwise indicated, all Scripture quotations are taken from *The Holy Bible*, English Standard Version (ESV). Copyright © 2001 by Crossway, a publishing ministry of Good News Publishers. Used by permission. All rights reserved.

Scripture quotations taken from the Amplified Bible (AMP). Copyright © 1954, 1958, 1962, 1964, 1965, 1987 by The Lockman Foundation. Used by permission. All rights reserved.

Scripture quotations taken from the God's Word Translation (GW). Copyright © 1995 by God's Word to the Nations. Used by permission of Baker Publishing Group. All rights reserved.

Scripture quotations taken from the King James Version (KJV)—public domain. Rights in the Authorized Version in the United Kingdom are vested in the Crown. Reproduced by permission of the Crown's patentee, Cambridge University Press.

Scripture quotations taken from The Living Bible (TLB). Copyright © 1971 by Tyndale House Foundation. Used by permission of Tyndale House Publishers Inc., Carol Stream, Illinois 60188. All rights reserved.

Scripture quotations taken from *The Message* (MSG). Copyright © 1993, 1994, 1995, 1996, 2000, 2001, 2002. Used by permission of NavPress Publishing Group.

Scripture quotations taken from the New American Standard Bible (NASB). Copyright © 1960, 1962, 1968, 1971, 1972, 1973, 1975, 1977, 1995 by The Lockman Foundation. Used by permission. All rights reserved.

Scripture quotations taken from the New King James Version (NKJV). Copyright © 1979, 1980, 1982 by Thomas Nelson, Inc. Used by permission. All rights reserved.

Cover Design by Benjamin Nolasco

www.thehappytrinity.com

Acknowledgments

There are so many people who have contributed to this book in so many little ways. Jesus, you saved my life from destruction and have never stopped loving me and having fun with me. Thank you for your broken body and your precious blood. Father, your joy gives me so much strength. I am so proud to be your child. Spirit, you are so amazing, you have so much energy, and you are always there to comfort me.

Whitney, my bride, you have made this gospel more real to me than I could have ever imagined. I married a missionary. Your conviction that you are loved by God is so strong that it changes atmospheres everywhere. Thank you for helping this book come to life. Many more adventures await us. To the nations!

Nick, you have been with me through thick and thin, and that's the real love of Jesus. Let's bring all of our lost brothers and sisters of Neverland back home.

To Mama Lani, thank you for showing me what this good news looks like. To Scott, thank you for making sure I actually have fun in real life and not just in my head. To Becky, thank you for being my sister and best friend. I will never stop believing in you. Mom, thank you for teaching me about Jesus and raising me in a happy home. Dad, thank you for teaching me the Italian spirit of celebration, joy, and family festivities. Grandpa is proud.

Debbie and Terry, you are the greatest in-laws I could have ever dreamed of. You are my best friends and you have shown me true love from day one. I'm so happy you're in my life. Grandma, thank you for praying for me my whole life. And Papa, can't wait to see you again and thank you for always being upset with the division between the Protestants and the Catholics. I'll keep working on that. And Uncle Lenny and Titi, my godparents, you taught me so much about happiness growing up. Uncle Lenny, thank you for showing me the funny, creative, story-telling side of Jesus.

And to all my friends and family, this book was also created by you. All the joy we've experienced together will never be forgotten but stands as a testimony to God's love forever. I'm so happy we get to be family forever in heaven. The good times are just beginning.

> *When the Lord restored the*
> *fortunes of Zion,*
> *we were like those who dream.*
> *Then our mouth was filled with laughter,*
> *and our tongue with shouts of joy ...*
> Psalm 126:1-2

Contents

Foreword	9
Introduction: To Know Him	11
Chapter One: The Trinity	19
Chapter Two: The Happiness of the Trinity	29
Chapter Three: The Laughter of the Trinity	45
Chapter Four: The Dance of the Trinity	55
Chapter Five: The Wrath of the Trinity	61
Chapter Six: The Grace of the Trinity	69
Chapter Seven: The Gospel of the Trinity	75
Chapter Eight: The Drink of the Trinity	83
Chapter Nine: The Apocalypse of the Happy Trinity	95
Epilogue: How Then, Shall We Live?	107

The Happy Trinity is her home; nothing can trouble her joy.
— C.S. Lewis, The Great Divorce

Foreword

Reading through Dylan's manuscript, I was impressed by both the tone of maturity it carries, as well as the subject matter. Just reading the Table of Contents, you can't help but have a big smile on your face! Happiness, Laughter, The Dance of the Holy Trinity ... WOW!

The Wrath of the Trinity is the title of one chapter. (What?! How is this subject matter included in this most joyful presentation?) But as I read that chapter, I was deeply impressed by Dylan DeMarsico's grasp of God's passion and desire to free humanity from all the destructive damage sin has caused. Giving to us His Son is the ultimate expression of the Father's creative passion (the true definition of God's wrath) to free His children from slavery. The Spirit causes us to experience the Trinity's overwhelming joy and celebration over what was accomplished as Christ and the believer were co-crucified, buried, and raised from the dead.

Dylan's own passion for his readers is that they too will experience and join this dancing, laughing Trinity who has truly rescued them from this present evil age. And that for the rest of our days on this earth we would be empowered

THE HAPPY TRINITY

to live in union with this glorious Trinity— demonstrating the really, really Good News of the Gospel! Fantastic job, Dylan!

— **Winnie "CoCo" Banov**
   Global Celebration
   www.globalcelebration.com

Introduction: To Know Him

In the days leading up the American Revolutionary War, when a fairly small group of people began to stand against the heavy burdens of an empire, a famous document was drafted called the Declaration of Independence. In this document was the mention of three inherent rights that were given by the Creator to each and every human being. These "rights" were described as "life, liberty, and the *pursuit of happiness*." Happiness was declared as something the Creator had called each person toward.

It is this God-given pursuit that we are looking at in the pages ahead.

But is this an elusive pursuit? Did God set us on an impossible path?

Where is happiness really found?

One thing is certain. *Everyone* is on this pursuit. Whether the drug addict, the billionaire, the porn star, or the priest, everyone is looking for happiness in their own way. Augustine, the ancient Church Father, once wrote, "Every man, whatsoever his condition, desires to be happy."[1] Even the person who commits suicide is looking for happiness. They just believe that they will find it through death.

Our hearts seek after it, sometimes for years, decades, maybe even our whole lives. Family and friends, great food and drink, sex, therapy, music…all these things may give us momentary comfort, but they still don't fulfill our heart's quest. This lack of fulfillment nags at us and causes us to ask the deepest questions of life.

Why do I exist? What's the point? Why am I here?

What do I have to do to be happy?

Will I ever be happy?

Am I even supposed to be happy?

Even in the church we fill our lives with many "good" things; be it prayer meetings, bible studies, outreaches, fasting, miracles, prophecies, and much more. All these things are fine but in and of themselves they fail to give rest to our souls. True and lasting peace is what our souls are looking for. We want to be happy. Not fake happy. Rather, a deep and true happiness in the deepest part of our beings.

The good news is that Jesus, the peaceful Revolutionary and great Redeemer, declared that each of us could *indeed find this happiness and rest*. He was certain that our deepest desires could be satisfied and that our "pursuit of happiness" was obtainable. Jesus said He came to give us this happiness and He called it "eternal life." And,

---

1. Thomas A. Hand, *St. Augustine on Prayer* (South Bend, IN: Newman Press, 1963), 1.

INTRODUCTION: TO KNOW HIM

surprisingly, He said that we would have "eternal life" by *knowing Him and His Father.*

> *"And this is eternal life, that they know You, the only true God, and Jesus Christ whom You have sent."*
> (John 17:3)

The most satisfying and happy life belongs to someone who *gets to know the living God.* If God is real and alive, well, what is He like? Does He talk? Is He in a good mood? Does He hate me? What does He think of me?

Is He happy with me?

To "Know" Christ

The apostle Paul wanted a true, happy, and fulfilled life as well. He claimed to have found the path and he expressed it by saying he had one purpose. In his letter to the Philippians, he lays this out with clarity, saying that his purpose was to get to know Jesus, the Messiah whom God had sent. He connected inner-fulfillment and happiness with getting to know Jesus (see Phil. 3:8).

But what does that mean? What does it look like to get to "know" Jesus?

Well, the Greek word for "know" is power-packed with layers upon layers of meaning. In the Amplified Bible, we can discover what Paul meant when he said he wanted to *know Christ*:

THE HAPPY TRINITY

> *"[For my determined purpose is] that I may know Him [that I may progressively become more deeply and intimately acquainted with Him, perceiving and recognizing and understanding the wonders of His Person more strongly and more clearly]."*
> (Philippians 3:10 AMP)

The Greek word to "know" is a word about *intimacy*. It is a Greek word that was often used to describe the intimacy between a man and a woman. This is talking about something that goes way beyond surface knowledge to a deep connectedness and awareness of another. Just as two people can share intimacy in a relationship, so too Paul wanted to know God in a deep and connected way. He wanted to be intimately acquainted with God—to *perceive, recognize, and understand* the wonders of Christ. And just like an intimate connection in a relationship brings happiness and pleasure, Paul expected these same things to come from His relationship with God.

Okay, but how? How do you get to know God on such an intimate level?

Do you just start talking to Him?

Yes, I'd definitely encourage you to start talking to Him, but I'd also encourage you to *learn* about Him so that you can *understand* what He is like. There's an ancient Proverb that says "understanding" is precious and valuable like silver and riches (Proverbs 2:4). To have

INTRODUCTION: TO KNOW HIM

"understanding" about God is more valuable than all the money in the world. Sure, money is great, and it's certainly important. However, no amount of money will ever give us true happiness.

The writer of Proverbs went on to say that if we seek understanding we'll find it and, more specifically, we'll find the "knowledge of God" (Proverbs 2:5). This "knowledge" is way more than mere facts in our heads. It might start there, but it ultimately leads to an awareness and intimate acquaintance with the Being who created you in your mother's womb. Getting to know God in this way infects the deepest places of your being, both the head and the heart.

The apostle Paul prayed for you. Did you know that? He prayed that you would be filled with the knowledge of God and have spiritual wisdom and understanding (Colossians 1:9-10). So, if we are serious about finding happiness, then let's embark on a journey to find the knowledge of God and get to know Him in an intimate way.

And where should we look first?

Jesus.

From the Father's Heart

God has spoken clearly through His one and only Son Jesus. The Old Testament was filled with shadows, prophecies, and dim light, but in the first century God opened wide the curtain:

THE HAPPY TRINITY

"Long ago, at many times and in many ways, God spoke to our fathers by the prophets, but in these last days he has spoken to us by His Son, whom He appointed the heir of all things, through whom He also created the world"
(Hebrews 1:1-2)

The ancient Jewish prophets were waiting and longing for the day when the Messiah would come. They prophesied of His coming and said it would be a time of great joy. Up until the Messiah's arrival the world was living in darkness and blindness. They had had encounters with God, but His full nature was still not all clear. According to the apostle John, nobody had ever seen God. But Jesus, the only Son, had known and seen God forever. John said that He came *straight from God the Father's heart* (see John 1:17).

And why did He come?

To make God known.

Good news: The very thing that we so desperately need—*to know God*—is the very thing that Jesus came to give us. God knew that our happiness would only come through knowing and encountering Him. Throughout human history, we have struggled to know God. We have created gods like Zeus or Molech and we've even tried to convince ourselves that *we* are God. But the *true happiness* that comes from knowing the *true God* has continued to elude us. Jesus is our only hope.

INTRODUCTION: TO KNOW HIM

Thankfully, Jesus came from God—full of grace and truth—in order to accomplish His work and introduce us to His Father. His blood has been poured out and He has risen from the grave in order to joyfully reveal God to us.

Leaving the Shire

In J.R.R. Tolkien's classic novel *The Lord of Rings*, there are a small group of characters called hobbits who are swept into a glorious and life-changing adventure. However, before they can begin their journey, they must first leave their comfortable home known as the Shire.[2]

The same goes for us right now. There may be places where we have grown comfortable with old and stale ideas about God. It is time to let those places go. We too are called to leave behind the Shire and take off on an adventure together—an adventure that leads to the *One who is far more precious than riches*. Our happiness can only be found in Him, and He is inviting us to play a game of Hide and Seek with Him.

Tag, you're it.

He's hiding. Start counting.

And maybe, just maybe, you'll see that He's easier to find than you thought…

---

[2]. Tolkien, J.R.R. The Fellowship of the Ring. New York: Houghton Mifflin Company, 1994. Print.

Chapter One: The Trinity

"The heavens were opened to Him and He saw the Spirit of God coming down in the form of a dove. And a voice from heaven said, 'This is my beloved Son, and I am wonderfully pleased with Him.'"
Matthew 3:17 (TLB)

One of the most striking things that Jesus revealed about God is that He is a relationship between a Father, His Son, and Their Spirit. That might sound odd at first, but with a little digging we will unearth an abundance of beauty, intimacy, and joy from this revelation. Understanding that God is a Trinity is foundational to discovering how happy He is. So let's go ahead and lay that foundation right now.

The Trinity in the Bible

The Bible makes clear the relationship between the Father, Son, and Spirit. Throughout the Scriptures, there is a real and dynamic conversation and friendship between the Three. Jesus's famous prayer to the Father in John 17 reveals great mysteries about this. One of them is the love that the Father had for the Son *before the world began*: "You loved Me before the foundation of the world," the Son spoke out to His Father (John 17:24).

Another scriptural example is the great affirmation the Father gives the Son at His baptism. A voice from heaven said, "This is My Beloved Son, with whom I am well pleased" (Matthew 3:17). These verses have to be taken at face value. *God, who is one in purpose and love, is diverse in His Personhood.*

Jesus spoke of the Spirit as a Person as well. He called Him the "Helper." The Gospel of John reads, "For if I do not go away, the Helper will not come to you. But if I go, I will send *Him* to you. And when *He* comes, *He* will convict the world concerning sin and righteousness and judgment" (John 16:7-8).

There are far more examples of the three Persons of the Trinity working together in the Bible: The Father *sent* the Son (John 3:16). The Spirit *searches* the depths of the Father and the Spirit *hears* from the Son (1 Corinthians 2:10 & John 16:13). The Son *praises* the Father and *sees* the Father doing things (Luke 10:19 & John 5:21). The list can go on and on. The main point here is that the Father, Son, and Spirit live in relationship with one another.

The early Christians accepted the truth that God the Father had sent God the Son to save the world, and, in the midst of it all, Their Spirit was at work. Paul finished his second letter to the Corinthians with this: "The grace of the Lord Jesus Christ, the love of God, and the communion of

CHAPTER ONE: THE TRINITY

the Holy Spirit be with all of you." Again, a clear reference to the three Persons of the Trinity.

For anyone who takes the Scriptures seriously, the three Persons of God is undeniable. Before God has a relationship with any of us, He has a relationship with Himself first. God is One Being of Power and Presence *in three Persons.* Next, let's take a quick look at the Nicene Creed.

The Nicene Creed

One of the most significant documents in all of church history was the Nicene Creed of 325 A.D. It was established by a council of church leaders and written to guard against false teachings. It affirmed not only what was in the Scriptures, but also what Christians continued to believe after the original apostles were martyred.

Before this creed was put together, there were many church leaders who believed in the Trinity. For example, Polycarp, a disciple of the apostle John, wrote, "O Lord God Almighty… I bless you and glorify you through the eternal and heavenly high priest Jesus Christ, your beloved Son, through whom be glory to you, with Him and the Holy Spirit, both now and forever."[3] You can see the Father, Son, and Spirit in Polycarp's reference.

Another example is Ignatius of Antioch, who was also a disciple of John in the late first century. He wrote, "In Christ Jesus our Lord, by Whom and with Whom be glory

---
3. Eddie Snipes, "Trinity: What the Early Church Believed" (Available online at http://www.highlandpc.com/studies/trinity.php).

and power to the Father with the Holy Spirit forever."[4] This is another clear reference from early Christianity.

All of this led to the construction of the famous Nicene Creed.[5] The creed lays out the reality of *one God in three Persons* with great clarity. It starts off with an affirmation of the Father:

> *"I believe in one God, the Father Almighty, Maker of heaven and earth, and of all things visible and invisible."*

The creed then continues with a statement about the Son:

> *"And in one Lord Jesus Christ, the only-begotten Son of God, begotten of the Father before all worlds; God of God, Light of Light, very God of very God; begotten, not made, being of one substance with the Father, by whom all things were made."*

And then of course, we read a description of the Person of the Holy Spirit:

> *"And I believe in the Holy Ghost, the Lord and Giver of Life; who proceeds from the Father and the Son; who with*

---

4. Eddie Snipes, "Trinity: What the Early Church Believed" (Available online at http://www.highlandpc.com/studies/trinity.php).

5. "Nicene Creed" (Available online at https://www.crcna.org/welcome/beliefs/creeds/nicene-creed).

CHAPTER ONE: THE TRINITY

the Father and the Son together is worshipped and glorified; who spoke by the prophets."

The creed is incredibly clear that the Father, Son, and Spirit is the *one* God whom we worship and glorify. This concept is unique to the Christian faith. Throughout the ages, the doctrine of the Trinity has been a central truth of the gospel of Jesus. There are innumerable examples through church history of the saints' belief in the Holy Trinity. Athanasius, Augustine, Martin Luther, and John Calvin are also amongst those who championed the teaching of the Father, Son, and Spirit.

So far, we're just scratching the surface. This is the groundwork for understanding the happiness of God. Let's begin to take a deeper look at how the three Persons of God relate to one another.

The Image of God

When we hear the phrase "the image of God," we most likely think of ourselves—humans. But one of the foundations of understanding the Trinity is that Christ, the Son, is the original image of God. Paul says it blatantly in 2 Corinthians 4:4 and Colossians 1:15 where he writes, "Christ, who is the image of God." The Son, you see, is the *reflection* or *self-image* that the Father has of Himself.

Jonathan Edwards, the famous 18th century theologian and revivalist, explained this beautifully when he wrote, "God perpetually and eternally has a most perfect idea of

Himself, as it were an exact image and representation of Himself ever before Him and in actual view."[6]

The Son was in the beginning with God as God's own Word, reflection, and exact imprint (John 1:1 & Hebrews 1:3). The Son is both a distinct Person from the Father and yet a direct extension of the Father as His perfect reflection and image.

You can think of it like this: The Son is the "selfie" of God. In the image of the Son, the Father sees Himself. But don't think that this means the Son is a static image. Jesus is a living and vibrant image of the Father. From all eternity, the Father has perfectly beheld this dynamic image that captures and glorifies His own beauty.

Contemporary pastor and author John Piper adds this: "Since the Son is the image of God and the radiance of God and the form of God, equal with God, and indeed *is* God, therefore God's delight in the Son is delight in Himself."[7] And that *delight* is where the Spirit comes into play. The Spirit is the love, peace, and joy that the Father and the Son have toward each other. So, the Father delights in His image, the Son, and the Spirit is the love that exists between the Father and the Son.

"You loved me before the foundation of the world!" This is what Jesus prayed to the Father in John 17. These words reveal the Father's eternal attitude toward the Son.

---

6. Jonathan Edwards, "An Essay on the Trinity" (Available online at https://www.ccel.org/ccel/edwards/trinity/files/trinity.html).

7. John Piper, *The Pleasures of God* (Portland, OR: Multnomah Press, 1991), 38.

CHAPTER ONE: THE TRINITY

There's never been a time when this was not true. The Father has always loved the Son. The Father's declaration, *"This is my Beloved Son with whom I am well pleased"*—which is what the Father said to the Son at His baptism—has been a reality from before the world began.

And the Spirit?

The Spirit was "hovering" over the waters in the beginning of creation (Genesis 1:1). In the same way, the Spirit is the movement, hovering, and the *act* of love from the Father to the Son, and vice versa. Edwards continues his examination of the Trinity: "An infinitely holy and sacred energy arises between the Father and Son in mutually loving and delighting in each other, for their love and joy is mutual…and there proceeds the third Person of the Trinity, the Holy Spirit, the Deity in act."[8] The Holy Spirit is the love, joy, and peace between the Father and Son.

It's also important to know that while the Spirit is indeed the love between the Father and Son, He is not just a mystical force. The Spirit is indeed a living Person. In fact, the Scriptures sometimes use feminine language and descriptions when discussing the *ruach* of God (the Hebrew word for "Spirit" is a *feminine* noun). In a way, the Holy Spirit is *like* the mother within the Trinity, giving us a complete image of a Divine Family—Father, Mother, and Son. This is never explicitly stated in Scripture; however, this comparison to a mother happens multiple times throughout the Bible.[9] It seems one of the only ways we can

---

8. Edwards, "Essay on the Trinity."
9. Matthew 23:37; Luke 15:8-10.

truly comprehend this miraculous dynamic of the Trinity is in how we understand human mothers and families.

To wrap all of this up, the Father has a perfect image, or reflection, of Himself. This reflection is the living Person of the Son. The Father, being the awesome, living God that He is, delights in His own glorious reflection in the Person of His Son. The energy, movement, and delight that is expressed between the Two is the Holy Spirit in each of Them. The Holy Spirit completes the circle, forming a divine and intimate Family of grace. These three Persons make up the One *being, nature, and essence* of God, who lives as *One* in the perfect unity of love, joy, and peace.

The Father's Delight

Let's look more closely at how the entire life of the Trinity begins with the Father's love toward His Son. This love within God is indeed a "perfect love" that casts out all fear (1 John 4:18). The Father's soul absolutely *delights* in His Son (Isaiah 42:1). Understand that all of this love is a *happy* love. It is a love that loves with the "fullness of joy" and with "pleasures forevermore" (see Psalm 16:11). As we just saw, the Father has been declaring, *"This is My Son whom I love with whom I am well-pleased"* forever!

The Greek word for "pleased" is directly related to "pleasure." All of the Father's *pleasure* is in His love for His Son, Jesus. All of His *delight* and *happiness* is focused on the eternal Son of God. As Jesus said in the gospel of John, "The Father loves the Son and has given all things into His hand" (John 3:35). There is such a special bond

CHAPTER ONE: THE TRINITY

between the Father and the Son. It's a mystery that we're blessed to even ponder.

The Father's love is eternally satisfied in Christ. The Father doesn't have mood swings within the Trinity but is infinitely happy with His Son Jesus. We must be very slow to compare God the Father with our earthly fathers. God is holy, and therefore He is different from our fathers. He is incredibly consistent in His love, which again, is rooted in Jesus. The Living Bible expresses the words of the Father beautifully:

> *"This is My beloved Son, and I am wonderfully pleased with Him!"*
> (Matthew 3:17)

This is the love that existed before the world began. To quote it one more time: Jesus said, "Father, you loved Me before the world began" (John 17:24). The Trinity teaches us that before the world was here, before we existed, the Father was already happy and pleased with His Son. Before this universe was birthed, there was *already* love, joy, and peace between the Father, Son, and Spirit.

These things that we are discussing are quite mysterious. They are so beautiful that our hearts and minds seem to light up with joy as we discover them. Sometimes, we seem to think that we are the creators of *love, joy, and peace*—as if God needed us to bring these fruits into the world. But actually, the opposite is true. Before the world began, before we were even here, these wonderful fruits of the Spirit were already fully in action in the Divine Family of the Trinity.

As we ponder all these things, here's a powerful statement right from the mouth of Jesus. In this passage, He invites each of us into the mysteries of the Trinity and His relationship with His Father:

> *"The Father has given me all these things to do and say. This is a unique Father-Son operation, coming out of Father and Son intimacies and knowledge. No one knows the Son the way the Father does, nor the Father the way the Son does. But I'm not keeping it to myself; I'm ready to go over it line by line with anyone willing to listen."*
> (Matthew 11:26-27 MSG)

And I have a hunch that you are *willing to listen…*

Chapter Two: The Happiness of the Trinity

"The beloved Son of God is [the Father's] most precious treasure, in which God's infinite happiness and joy, from eternity to eternity, does consist."[10]
Jonathan Edwards

The basis for God's happiness is so simple: He lives in the relationship of the Trinity. God has never been alone, nor has He ever been bored. He has forever lived in relationship as the Father, Son, and Spirit. There is more happiness in the Trinity than we could possibly fathom, even if we took a billion years to think it over.

C.S. Lewis described this happiness of the Trinity in his classic allegory *The Great Divorce*. He wrote, "The Happy Trinity is her home: nothing can trouble her joy."[11] He was explaining that the Trinity is *happy* and that we can

---

10. Jonathan Edwards, "Notes on the Bible: Exodus," *The Works of Jonathan Edwards,* vol. 2.

11. C.S. Lewis, *The Great Divorce* (New York, NY: HarperCollins Publishers, 1946), 134.

make our home there. The Trinity's happiness is stable and consistent. It doesn't fluctuate like weak human emotions do. That's what makes God so amazing: His faithfulness to His happiness.

The idea of God being *happy* seems odd; however, because God is a Trinity, this is not that hard to understand. The Father, Son, and Spirit *enjoy* each other's company. Though this might even sound like a totally new idea, there are many people throughout church history who have recognized God's happiness.

The influential pastor and author A.W. Tozer wrote, "God is not only pleased with Himself, delighted with His own perfection and happy in His work of creating and redeeming, but He is also enthusiastic. There is an enthusiasm in the Godhead, and there is enthusiasm in creation… This infinite God is enjoying Himself. Somebody is having a good time in heaven and earth."[12]

Another, John Bunyon, author of *The Pilgrim's Progress*, wrote, "God is the chief good… He is in Himself most happy…and all true happiness is only to be found in God, as that which is essential to His nature."[13] Bunyon further points out that there is only one happiness in the world, and that is *God's happiness*. Sometimes we think we have to create our own happiness, but God invites us to freely join and share in *His happiness*.

---

12. A.W. Tozer, *Knowledge of the Holy* (New York, NY: HarperCollins, 1961), 10-13.

13. John Bunyan, "Christ: A Complete Saviour," *The Works of John Bunyon*, vol. 1.

CHAPTER TWO: THE HAPPINESS OF THE TRINITY

Even the future of the world is very much connected to happiness. The Psalmist writes, "The Lord reigns, let the earth be glad" (Psalm 97:1). This is so much more than a nice blurb on a Christmas greeting card! The earth will *actually be glad one day.* And it will all be due to the fact that *the Lord reigns.* Jonathan Edwards furthered this biblical sentiment when he wrote, "Happiness is the end [purpose] of the creation… For certainly it was the goodness of the Creator that moved Him to create…that He might delight in seeing the creatures He made rejoice."[14] God's plan is that heaven and earth find great happiness in Him!

Happiness and Joy

Many people are afraid of God—and it's not the good kind of fear that brings a reverential awe. It's the fear that keeps people from approaching their Creator. Some people would never think that God is *happy*. They would have a hard time believing that He smiles or laughs. Yet the question of whether or not God is happy is at the core of our spiritual journey. And indeed, the answer to that question is both shocking and beautiful.

There is a great deal of books about the Person of God, but sadly there are only a very few that cover God's *happiness*. We hear about grace, love, power, justice, wrath, and many other attributes of God, all of which are wonderful and essential. Yet somehow a simple understanding of God's happiness has slipped under the

---

14. Jonathan Edwards, *A Jonathan Edwards Reader* (New Haven, CT: Yale University Press, 1995), 36-37.

radar. This is surprising considering the Bible is full of passages about the divine gladness.

First off, let's quickly discuss the word *happy*. It sounds like an "unspiritual" word, but according to history and the Bible, happiness is essential to a relationship with God. Contemporary author Randy Alcorn wrote a whole book about God called *Happiness*. He gives thousands of examples from the Bible, Jewish history, and church history as to why the word *happy* is a great word to ascribe to God and believers.

At one point in his book, Alcorn asks, "What's the difference between joy and happiness?"[15] And it turns out: nothing! Almost every English dictionary, both secular and Christian, defines "joy" as a "state of happiness." Webster's dictionary defines joy as "a feeling of great happiness."

Alcorn points out that it was Oswald Chambers who popularized the difference between joy and happiness in the 20th century.[16] Chambers wrote that it was an "insult to Jesus Christ to use the word happiness in connection with Him."[17] Even though Chambers' heart may have been in the right place and his book is a classic that has helped many people, this severing of joy and happiness is neither historical nor biblical.

---

15. Randy Alcorn, *Happiness* (Carol Stream, IL: Tyndale House, 2015), 35.
16. Alcorn, *Happiness*, 39.
17. Oswald Chambers, *My Utmost for His Highest* (Grand Rapids, MI: Discovery House, 2006), 31.

CHAPTER TWO: THE HAPPINESS OF THE TRINITY

Alcorn ends up pointing out the obvious: "Happiness is joy. Joy is happiness. Virtually all dictionaries, whether secular or Christian, recognize this."[18]

John Piper also wrote about the "difference" between joy and happiness: "If you have nice little categories for 'joy is what Christians have' and 'happiness is what the world has,' you can scrap those when you go to the Bible, because the Bible is indiscriminate in its use of the language of happiness and joy and contentment and satisfaction."[19]

So then, in the pages ahead you will see the words *joy* and *happiness* used interchangeably. They cover the same reality: the state of being happy, cheerful, smiley, content, and feeling good! This is important, because it's silly to pretend that God is joyful in some "fancy-spiritual" sense but not in a "smile-on-his-face-happy" sense. Happiness is joy and joy is happiness and we don't have to pretend otherwise.

The Jewish Understanding of God's Happiness

The ancient Hebrews recognized that God was a glad God. Go all the way back to the creation account. We know that the Holy Trinity was all there when it says, "Let *Us* make man in *Our* image" (Genesis 1:26). After each day, the Trinity made stuff and God *saw that it was good*. The

---

18. Alcorn, *Happiness*, 42.

19. John Piper, "Let Your Passion be Single," Desiring God, November 12, 1999, http://desiringgod.org/conference-messages/let-your-passion-be-single.

THE HAPPY TRINITY

Living Bible translates each part of Genesis 1 as saying, "And God was pleased."

From the beginning, there was this Divine pleasure that jumps out at us. Even the garden itself was called *Eden*, which is a Hebrew word that means "delight" and "pleasure." It was painstakingly obvious to the ancient Jews that God was a happy God. This was in contrast to other ancient creation stories where the universe was created because of a war between angry deities.

Many of the Jewish prophets had tasted of heavenly joy as well. David proudly wrote in Psalm 18, "He delivered me because He delighted in me." David knew that God's deliverance was motivated by delight and joy. The prophet Isaiah said that God would rejoice over His people like a bridegroom rejoices over His bride" (Isaiah 62:5)!

Jeremiah said that God would do good to His people. But not just "good" in a "God-is-good-so-He-is-supposed-to-do-good" way. Jeremiah said that God would "rejoice in doing them good" with *all of His heart and soul* (see Jeremiah 32:41). God actually enjoys being good! In fact, His goodness toward His people is simply the overflow of His happiness!

One objection to the happiness of God in the Old Testament is related to all of the judgments spoken by the prophets. But there is one common theme in all of the Old Testament prophets…

> *…all of their proclamations of judgment were always about leading people back to joy!*

CHAPTER TWO: THE HAPPINESS OF THE TRINITY

Take Jeremiah for example. He laid out many judgments on Israel for their idol-worship and rebellion. Yet, as the aforementioned verse states, it was all leading to a future where God would rejoice in His people with all of His heart and soul (Jeremiah 32:41).

We'll look more into this later, but suffice it to say that God's judgments were always temporary acts that were meant to lead His people back to the happiness of knowing Him. Like a good Father, He set firm boundaries in place, such as the command to stay away from idols. But this was precisely because He knew our happiness could not be found in them. In fact, these things only suck the life out of us and destroy any lasting peace and joy in our lives.

God was always working toward leading His people back to Himself—back to the source of true joy. This was the delightful understanding of the Jewish people as seen in the 97th Psalm. God's judgments led to joy:

> *Zion heard this and **was glad**,*
> *And the daughters of Judah have rejoiced*
> ***Because of Your judgments**, O Lord.*
> (Psalm 97:10 NASB)

The Son's Extreme Joy

The Son of God, as we've found out, is the perfect image and reflection of the Father. Therefore, the Son is an extremely happy Person as well. The Psalmist and the author of Hebrews declares that the Father anoints the Son with the "oil of gladness" beyond His companions

(Hebrews 1:9). Strong's concordance of the Bible indicates that the Greek word "gladness" in this verse could be translated as "extreme joy."[20]

Taking a cue from Hebrews 1:9, John Piper wrote, "Jesus Christ is the happiest being in the universe. His gladness is greater than all the angelic gladness of heaven. He mirrors perfectly the infinite, holy, indomitable mirth of His Father."[21]

Is it surprising to think that Jesus is not only filled with joy, but *extreme* joy? Let's think about it from a biblical perspective. While His heart certainly breaks for the pain and hurt in this world, Jesus has completed His work on the cross and has been raised from the dead by His Father. He is now seated at His Father's right hand, and is drawing the world to Himself by His Spirit. Heaven is filled with so much joy and excitement, and now every time a sinner repents, all of heaven erupts in celebration (Luke 15). Jesus, the One who is the source of all joy, leads this ongoing celebration in His Father's house.

Think about the power that it takes for God to hold the entire universe together. Now think about the power with which the Father loves His Son. The Son is loved with an absolutely infinite love that could never be contained. The Father's love holds millions of galaxies in orbit. *That's* the love that the Father so perfectly has for His Son.

---

20. "Lexicon: Strong's G20: *Agalliasis*" (https://www.blueletterbible.org/lang/lexicon/lexicon.cfm?Strongs=G20&t=KJV).

21. John Piper, *Seeing and Savoring Jesus Christ* (Wheaton, IL: Crossway, 2004), 36.

CHAPTER TWO: THE HAPPINESS OF THE TRINITY

And that's what makes the Son of God such an extremely joyful Person. We assume that Jesus's joy depends on humanity's performance. *But a revelation of the Trinity banks Jesus's joy on the rock-solid fact of His Father's almighty love for Him.* Being delighted in by the All-Powerful Father is the source of Jesus's extreme joy.

19th century pastor Charles Spurgeon once said, "The joy of Jesus is, first, the joy of abiding in His Father's love. He knows that His Father loves Him…that is the joy which Christ gives to you – the joy of knowing that your Father loves you…even as Jesus Christ is loved."[22]

Jesus's joy does not waver; it does not go up and down based on our performance. His joy is perfect and full because His Father loves Him perfectly. Always remember that the Father's love and delight in His Son is also a love and delight in *Himself.* Again, this is because the Son is the image and reflection of the Father. It is like a proud father who takes pride in himself because of how wonderful His child is.

If you ever begin to question God's happiness, remember that it begins with the Father's love for the Son. This is why the fact that God is a Trinity is such good news. The Father delights in His Son with all His heart. The Son rejoices exceedingly in His Father's love. Being perfectly loved *and being able to perfectly receive that love* is what makes the Son an extremely joyful Person. The Spirit is the One who jumps back and forth between the two in Their

---

22. Charles H. Spurgeon, "Christ's Joy and Ours" (Sermon #2935).

perfect fellowship and unending joy. The Trinity, without any help from us, is happy beyond our wildest imagination.

The Entertainment and Fun of God

Earlier, we looked at some of the mysteries contained within Jesus's prayer to the Father when He said, "You loved me before the foundation of the world" (John 17:24). At this point we need to go back to those words and unpack even more treasure from them. We'll do this by looking once more at the Greek word for love—*agape*.

The word has a few meanings to it. Part of the word means to "welcome." So the Father has "welcomed" the Son from all eternity. But another key meaning of this word is "to entertain."

That's right, you read correctly. *Loving* somebody is connected with *entertaining* that person. Think about the love that is needed to love orphan children. Yes, feeding them food and providing for them is most important. But also, providing *joyful entertainment* brings their hearts to life as well. The biblical definition of love is packed with abundant life and glorious excitement!

To say that the Father *loved* His Son before the world began is also to say that He *entertained* His Son before the universe was here. Yes, the Father has eternally provided for His Son, but it's not like They were bored for all eternity just sitting around! They weren't just "loving" one another in a dry and monotonous sense.

CHAPTER TWO: THE HAPPINESS OF THE TRINITY

Now what do you think the Father's entertainment is like? Certainly, it must be a rich and exhilarating entertainment that causes awe and wonder in its audience! Just like in the books of Exodus and Acts, there is a "wow-factor" that God seems to delight in.

Think about it. This was definitely in God's mind when He created Adam and Eve and put them in the Garden of pleasure—Eden. In a very real way, humanity was made to be "entertained" in this Garden of delight. God made all the unique and beautiful trees of the Garden to be "pleasant to the sight" (Genesis 2:9). Now consider the entertainment of the world—things like movies and video games are created to be "pleasant to the sight."

This helps us to understand that entertainment itself is not evil. It is simply a reflection of what God is like. And since we are made in the "image" or "reflection" of God, we are simply doing what we were created to do. Of course, things can be twisted by evil; however, wholesome entertainment that makes us have more awe and wonder is vital.

Think of the ways in which humans entertain each other: songs, music, dancing, games, movies, shows, sports, good food, comedy, etc. These entertaining activities of mankind reflect the entertainment of the Father and His Son with Their Spirit!

It's possible that Jesus hinted at this divine entertainment when He said there was "music and dancing" in the Father's house (Luke 15:25). In the parable of the prodigal son, Jesus included that little detail. He said the Father

THE HAPPY TRINITY

welcomed the son back home and threw a party where there was music and dancing.

Jesus had likely known the happy music and dancing of the Father from all eternity. He came to reveal the Father and He made sure to include the fun and entertaining side of God too!

Even the concept of "fun" can certainly be found in the Trinity according to the Bible. The dictionary defines "fun" as "enjoyment or lighthearted pleasure."[23] Enjoyment and pleasure are at the heart of the gospel. Look at this statement from the book of Revelation: "For thou hast created all things, and for *Thy pleasure* they are and were created" (Revelation 4:11 KJV)!

In a very real sense, according to the Scriptures, it would be theologically correct to say that the Trinity created all things for "fun." This "fun" is the enjoyment and pleasure that we were created to share with our Father. If we could travel back in time and hang out with the early church, we would be surprised that they too were having a lot of fun. Yes, they were serious about the gospel of Christ, but taking the gospel seriously meant surrendering to God's enjoyment and pleasure. It meant being free in the joy of the Lord (see Philippians 4:4)!

This joy and "fun" of the Lord was the disciples' strength (see Nehemiah 8:10). It empowered them to love their enemies, forgive those who persecuted them, and even give their lives to martyrdom. Miserable people don't

---

23. Google Dictionary, "Fun" (Available online at https://www.google.com/search?q=Dictionary#dobs=fun).

CHAPTER TWO: THE HAPPINESS OF THE TRINITY

give up their own lives, but people filled with the joy of Jesus will willingly lay down their lives for the cause of the gospel. In this age, we have nothing to fear. Even if we die, we will immediately be with the Trinity in heaven (Philippians 1:23).

The First Century Christians

Saying that God is *extremely happy* might sound like a new or offensive idea. But this really is nothing new. First century Christians discovered a God of *good news*. When they prayed, they were praying to a God who they believed was enormously happy in all His power, love, and glory.

First century Christians believed that Christ was in them. Jesus was their indwelling life. And what were they marked by? They were marked by *joy*. Even in the midst of terrible persecution, they were an abundantly happy bunch. Paul and Silas were singing songs to God while in prison for preaching the gospel! Of course, there are always difficult times in life, and we don't have to be in denial about that, but true Christ-like life is filled with happiness.

Paul told the early believers, "Rejoice in the Lord always; again I will say, rejoice" (Philippians 4:4). Notice the small phrase "in the Lord." The joy that Paul encourages his disciples to tap into is a divine joy. It's the very joy of Jesus Himself. We don't have to try and produce our own joy. We are recipients of a joy that is in the heart of Jesus. The sharing of His joy is one of the main reasons Jesus came to earth: "That they may have My joy fulfilled in themselves" (John 17:13).

THE HAPPY TRINITY

For the first believers, being Christ-like and being joyful were completely compatible because they knew that Christ was always rejoicing in His Father's love! This was at the heart of what they believed! They believed that Jesus was the chosen One of God, totally delighted in by God the Father. They knew they were believing in an incredibly happy Savior.

The first sermon ever preached on Jesus was by the apostle Peter on the day of Pentecost when the Holy Spirit came like the wind. There's something deeply important in this sermon that can get easily overlooked. In this message by Peter, when he preached to thousands of people from all over the world, he spoke about Jesus being glad, joyful, and happy three different times. And this was a foundational sermon for the entire future church of Jesus Christ!

In the sermon, Peter quoted Psalm 16 to describe Jesus. He goes out of his way to say that David was not speaking about himself in the Psalm, but about Christ, the Messiah (Acts 2:29). Peter said that Jesus's *heart was glad* and His *tongue rejoiced* in His faith in the Father who raised Him from the dead (Acts 2:26). He went on to say that the Father raised Jesus from the dead and made Him *full of gladness* in the Father's presence (Acts 2:28)! Can you imagine being there for that original sermon? The authority on the apostle Peter to boldly proclaim a glad and rejoicing Savior who was raised from the dead by God! It's no wonder they were pierced to the heart.

From the very beginning of the church, the apostles preached about the Father, the Son, the Holy Spirit, and

CHAPTER TWO: THE HAPPINESS OF THE TRINITY

Their over-the-top gladness and victory. When the first gospel audience heard the good news, they were cut to the heart because the message of God's goodness is *painful* to realize after living a life in the misery of sin, depression, and evil. The repentance that the apostles demanded was for the people to turn from sin to a God who was celebrating Jesus's resurrection with abundant joy.

We cannot pretend as though God's joy over Christ's victory was not at the center of the original Christian message. Furthermore, it's utterly clear that as thousands upon thousands of men, women, and children began to believe the gospel, there was an eruption of joy all over the place. From before time began, to the Jewish understanding of God, to the birth of the church, joy has always been central to God's message.

Let's continue to explore more of the depths of this faithful and eternal joy.

Chapter Three: The Laughter of the Trinity

"I was His constant delight, laughing and playing in His presence. And how happy I was with what He created—His wide world and all His family of mankind!"
Proverbs 8:30-31 (TLB)

So far, we have made the rich discovery that in the presence of God there is *fullness of joy* (Psalm 16:11). The Hebrew word for fullness means "abundance" and "to the full." When God expresses Himself, it comes from this place of abundant and overflowing joy.

But what is the sound of that expression? What does this overflow look like?

Laughter!

The living God is a God of laughter. Laughter is the sound or expression of joy. It is what happens when happiness overflows from within. Is it surprising then that God is a Father, Son, and Spirit who are abundant in laughter?

THE HAPPY TRINITY

Meister Eckhart, a 14th century German theologian, was a Christian who gazed into the mystery of the Trinity. He discovered the divine fullness of joy and gave a metaphoric picture of the Trinity. He said, "In the heart of the Trinity the Father laughs and gives birth to the Son. The Son laughs back at the Father and gives birth to the Spirit. The whole Trinity laughs and gives birth to us!"[24]

In the Beginning was Laughter

But what do the Scriptures say about this laughter? Where in the Bible can we find God laughing? Come with me to a glorious passage in Proverbs 8…

In this chapter we meet Wisdom, who describes what it was like to be with God at the creation of the world. We learn from other Scriptures that Wisdom is a personification of Christ. In the New Testament, Christ is directly called "the wisdom of God" (1 Corinthians 1:30). In this passage from Proverbs, Wisdom tells us what He[25] and God were doing in the beginning of the earth's construction:

> *When He marked out the foundations of the earth, then I was beside Him, like a master workman, and I was daily His delight, rejoicing before Him always,*

---

24. "Laughter and God - Meister Eckhart" (Available online at http://www.societyofsacredheart.org/spirituality/laughter-and-god?start=1).

25. Proverbs uses the female pronoun in this passage; however, it can still be connected to Christ, because He used female pronouns to describe Himself and His Father multiple times. See Matthew 23:37 and Luke 15:8-10.

CHAPTER THREE: THE LAUGHTER OF THE TRINITY

rejoicing in His inhabited world and
delighting in the children of man.
(Proverbs 8:30-31)

So here we see God the Son (Wisdom) with God the Father creating all things. This completely lines up with the rest of Scripture:

In the beginning was the Word and the
Word was with God.
(John 1:1)

All things have been created through Him
and for Him.
(Colossians 1:16)

In Proverbs 8, we see Christ as the delight of God, *rejoicing always* before Him, rejoicing in the world and delighting in humans—us! Here's the thing though: the Hebrew word for "rejoicing" really means something else. "Rejoicing" is a conservative translation.

The Hebrew word is *sachaq*, which means "to laugh" and "to play."[26]

It seems that some of the serious and mature Bible translators out there just couldn't bring themselves to say that God was laughing and playing when He made the world. If God was laughing and playing, then there's some theological seminary books that might need to be updated!

---

26. "Lexicon: Strong's H7832: *Sachaq*" (https://www.blueletterbible.org/lang/lexicon/lexicon.cfm?Strongs=H7832&t=KJV).

THE HAPPY TRINITY

The Living Bible translates it more accurately than most translations. Here it is again, with some more context:

> *I was there when He made the blueprint for the earth and oceans. I was always at His side like a little child. I was His constant delight, laughing and playing in His presence. And how happy I was with what He created – His wide world and all His family of mankind!*
> (Proverbs 8:29-31 TLB)

Now that's more like it! Let's give a big round of applause to the translators of the Living Bible for having the guts to translate that passage correctly.

This passage teaches us that the Father, Son, and Spirit were laughing and playing as They created the universe. The picture portrayed is of the Father delighting and rejoicing in the Son as He laughs and plays before Him. In His laughter and play, God both purposely and spontaneously creates the earth, the oceans, the hills, the waters, men, women, zebras, elephants, giraffes, monkeys, pineapples, bumblebees, air, and everything else in the cosmos.

How have you imagined the creation of the world? For most people it is very vague. But the Scriptures offer us something so filled with life. The family of the Trinity was laughing, playing, rejoicing and delighting in one another as They speak forth this world.

CHAPTER THREE: THE LAUGHTER OF THE TRINITY

Take a deep breath and realize that you are the product of Someone who laughs and plays. Maybe close the book and take a few more deep breaths and pray to your Father in heaven who knit you together in His loving laughter. Let any fear, shame, or guilt be swallowed up in His joy.

Truly, the world was birthed out of the laughter of God. The Trinity, in the fullness of Their joy, overflowed in laughter and... well, here we are. It is this kind of over-the-top joy and laughter that is God's strength (Nehemiah 8:10). Yes, the joy of the Lord is His strength too! This is no mere Sunday School lesson. It's this almighty and all-powerful laughter that contained the force to create all things.

Sports and the Play of the Trinity

Proverbs 8 amazingly shows us that God was laughing and *playing* when He made the universe. The fact that the Father and Son were "playing" at creation gives immense weight and value to the significance of "play" in our own lives. Randy Alcorn writes, "Play is happiness in motion."[27] Any good father on earth *plays* with his kids. How much more does the Father who is filled with the fullness of joy play with His children?

Understanding that God plays helps us to make sense of why sports are so popular in this world. In every

---
27. Alcorn, *Happiness*, 170.

nation, there are sports. Throughout the world, soccer, or "football," is the main sport that everyone plays. There are hundreds of millions in America and the world who love basketball, baseball, and football. In Canada, hockey is the national sport. Every four years, multitudes of nations come together to *play games* during the Olympics.

So are sports just an evil invention of humanity? Do they arise from a competitive part of the sinfulness amongst man to one-up one another?

Like anything else, good things can be corrupted; nevertheless, corruption does not negate the original value of something. In fact, it only points to the fact that something quite pure and beautiful lies underneath. If we are made in the image of God, then playing sports is us *reflecting our Father.* We were created to play just like the Father, Son, and Spirit play.

This is why some people, particularly husbands and fathers, are big fans of sports. Without realizing it, they are looking for their heavenly Father who plays. Sports are an outlet where people are actually seeking the God who plays! Some people get addicted to watching sports as an escape from life. If only they encountered their Father who plays, they wouldn't need an escape and would learn to have a healthy balance.

When we understand that God is playing all the time, we are empowered to "play" all throughout life. Instead of just trudging along in the boredoms of life, God's happiness inspires us to play with our families, friends, and co-workers. Again, play is simply "happiness in motion."

CHAPTER THREE: THE LAUGHTER OF THE TRINITY

An Everlasting Laughter

Let's get back to the creation of the world. We need to understand something else about all this talk of God's joy. The laughter and play of God was not a one-time event where He created the world and then stopped and left everything to run on its own.[28] It's not as if God laughed and played when creating the world and then over time He lost excitement, and is now bored or indifferent. Look at this unbelievable quote from the great Christian author G.K. Chesterton about God's continual creation of the world:

"Because children have abounding vitality, because they are in spirit fierce and free, therefore they want things repeated and unchanged. They always say, 'Do it again'; and the grown-up person does it again until he is nearly dead. For grown-up people are not strong enough to exult in monotony. But perhaps God is strong enough to exult in monotony. It is possible that God says every morning, 'Do it again' to the sun; and every evening, 'Do it again' to the moon. It may not be automatic necessity that makes all daisies alike; it may be that God makes every daisy separately, but has never got tired of making them. It may be that He has the eternal appetite of infancy; for we have sinned and grown old, and our Father is younger than we."[29]

The Father, Son, and Spirit are still creating the world every day. They are still laughing and playing as They

---

28. The belief in a God who created the world but then left it to run on its own is called Deism. It's not Christian at all. God continues to sustain the world every day in His joy.

29. G.K. Chesterton, *Orthodoxy* (The Project Gutenberg e-Book, 1994), 143.

sustain all things. Paul clearly taught that the Father is still sustaining all things through the Son (Colossians 1:17). The breath in your lungs, the heartbeat in your chest, your dog running around; all these things are sustained and created by the continual joy of the Lord.

This truth is blatantly found in Psalm 104. This is a Psalm about all the details of the ongoing creation. The waves of the sea, the chirping of the birds, and the deer drinking water; the Psalmist describes all of this and then attributes it to the work of God. Then he writes something remarkable:

> *May the glory of the Lord endure forever;*
> *may the Lord rejoice in His works.*[30]
> (Psalm 104:31)

This Psalm provides a picture of the living God who is rejoicing as He causes all of creation to move and animate. With fullness of joy and overflowing laughter, God is continually enjoying all the things that He does. And of course, this includes *all things*. He sustains every single detail of life in this universe and He rejoices and laughs through it all.

---

30. John Piper explains in *The Pleasures of God (p. 86)*, that the Psalmist isn't requesting that God rejoice in His works but making a statement of certainty. Piper says that this verse means something like, "As long as the *glory* of the Lord endures in his works, God will indeed *rejoice* in His works."

CHAPTER THREE: THE LAUGHTER OF THE TRINITY

His Laughter in Redemption

And not only that, but it's this laughter that overflows into grace towards humanity, which is something we'll explore in more depth soon enough. Joy moved Jesus to the cross and drove God to not count humanity's sins against them (Hebrews 12:2 & 2 Corinthians 5:20). It was out of this divine pleasure that God chose to freely forgive humanity and make her holy and blameless before Him in love. Paul taught clearly in Ephesians that it was God's *pleasure* to save us (Ephesians 1:5 NKJV). The abundance of God's joy was the reason He was so generous in taking away the sins of the world through Christ.

God's laughter has always stayed true. "For I the Lord do not change," God declared through the voice of a prophet (Malachi 3:6). In spite of humanity's sin and their evil plots against Him, *God's laughter has never stopped.* "Why do the nations rage, and the peoples plot in vain… He who sits in the heavens laughs" (Psalm 2:1, 4). No evil that humans create can stop God from being Himself. His joy is stronger than evil and death.

It comes back to a simple truth, that even when humanity sins, God's joy proves stronger and greater. And this is certainly not a distant or mocking joy. Jesus is also the one who mourns with those who mourn and weeps over our pain. Nonetheless, His laughter and happiness still bursts through the fog bringing clarity and renewal. His laughter is actually what heals our weeping! Even the book of Proverbs teaches that a cheerful heart is like medicine (see Proverbs 17:22).

THE HAPPY TRINITY

In a million ways, God has proven to be greater than the evil of this world. It's His joyful love that empowered Him to stoop down and show compassion, to take on the sin of the world, and to overcome death. When Peter quoted Psalm 16 in that first sermon of church history, he was proclaiming the power of God's gladness over sin, misery, and death. In describing the resurrection of Jesus, Peter said, "You will make Me full of gladness with Your Presence" (Acts 2:28)!

How incredible is that? It's that same *fullness of joy* and *laughter* that raised Jesus from the dead and raised the world to new life in Him. And it's that same *good* pleasure that will continue to gather up all things in Christ until the earth is filled with the knowledge of the glory of the Lord)![31]

---

31. Here are some of the glorious Scriptures that the above paragraph is built upon: Ephesians 2:5-6; Ephesians 1:10-11; Habakkuk 2:14

Chapter Four: The Dance of the Trinity

"He happily rejoices over you, renews you with his love, and celebrates over you with shouts of joy."
Zephaniah 3:17 (GW)

Oftentimes, when humans are happy, they *dance*. In light of our excursions into the nature of God, this begs a certain question: If God, the One whose image we bear, is filled with joy…then does He dance as well?

Of course, the answer is yes!

He Dances for Joy

This becomes glaringly obvious when you look at some of the words from the prophet Zephaniah. He writes that God "is a mighty Savior. He will give you victory. He will rejoice over you in great gladness; He will love you and not accuse you. Is that a joyous choir I hear? No, it is the Lord Himself exulting over you in happy song" (Zephaniah 3:17 TLB).

Once again, some of the Hebrew words in this passage have deeper meanings that are not fully captured in the English. One word is "rejoice," which in this instance comes from the Hebrew word *suws*. This word can be translated as "rejoice," but it can also mean to "leap or spring."[32] This word shows us that God's joy leads Him to *leap and spring!* Perhaps this is why Jesus taught His disciples to "leap for joy"—because He does it too! (Luke 6:23)

Another important word in this passage is "exult." This comes from the Hebrew *giyl*. This word is a doozy! The Hebrew definition of the word is, "to spin around under the influence of violent emotion."[33] Wow!

The God of the universe spins around and dances for joy over us!

This is the living God that has revealed Himself through Christ. The Father dances around under the influence of violent emotion. The word is used again in Isaiah 65 when God says that He will "rejoice" over Jerusalem (or *spin around in violent emotion* over the city). The book of Hebrews tells us we belong to the heavenly Jerusalem (Hebrews 12:22). That means our Father is dancing and spinning around us right now!

---

32. "Lexicon: Strong's H7797: *Suws*" (https://www.blueletterbible.org/lang/lexicon/lexicon.cfm?Strongs=H7797&t=KJV).

33. "Lexicon: Strong's H1523: *Giyl*" (https://www.blueletterbible.org/lang/lexicon/lexicon.cfm?Strongs=H1523&t=KJV).

CHAPTER FOUR: THE DANCE OF THE TRINITY

The Scriptures teach us that God is like a bridegroom and we are like a bride. His dancing is filled with love and delight. Isaiah caught this when he prophesied, "For the Lord delights in you… for as a young man marries a young woman…and as the bridegroom rejoices over the bride, so shall your God rejoice over you" (Isaiah 62:4-5).

The Triune Dance

Some of the ancient believers taught that the Trinity *is* a dance. To teach this, they used a Greek word *perichoresis*, which means "rotation." The earliest teacher to possibly use the term in connection to the Godhead was Cyril of Alexandria, a 4th and 5th century Bishop in the city of Alexandria.[34] He also served on the Council of Ephesus in 431 A.D. Perichoresis teaches that the Trinity can be understood *as a rotation of love between the Father, Son, and Spirit.*

To explain it further, God is love and we know that love is self-giving. The Father is always giving Himself to the Son, the Son is always giving Himself to the Father, and the Spirit is always giving Himself to the Father and the Son. Around and around it goes, ceaseless and vibrant. This is the rotation of the Trinity, or the dance of God's love.

Dancing was going on when the Father threw a party for the prodigal son. Jesus said there was "music and dancing" in the Father's house (Luke 15:25). Jesus depicted His Father's party with music and dancing for us

---

34. Trinity in You, "What is Perichoresis?" (Available online at http://trinityinyou.com/welcome-to-trinity-in-you/19-2/).

to realize how abundant God's love is. He wanted us to see that the Father's love is not stagnant, but full of life. The gospel brings us into the Trinity's dance! The rotation of love now includes us!

There's not only dancing in the Trinity, but singing too! The author of Hebrews wrote that Jesus *sings* to His Father. He quotes Jesus saying to the Father, "I will declare your name to My brothers; in the presence of the congregation I will sing your praises" (Hebrews 2:12). Jesus sings to the Father in our presence!

The Dance of the Spirit

But what exactly is dancing? That might seem like a rudimentary question, but let's really think about this. Dancing is the movement of the body, and it usually involves music.

Now, right in the beginning of the Scriptures, we learn that the Spirit of God was *moving* or *hovering* over the surface of the deep (Genesis 1:2). And in the book of Job we discover that when God created the world, there was music and song (see Job 38:7). In some ways, we can see that God's Spirit was *moving to music at creation*. The Spirit was likely moving to the rhythm of God's song.

The Holy Spirit is a mover. He shakes and hovers and rushes around like wind. Throughout the Scriptures, the Spirit is like a wild dancer who is extremely unpredictable. In the beginning, He was moving over the earth and *He hasn't stopped moving since*. But this "moving" isn't

CHAPTER FOUR: THE DANCE OF THE TRINITY

chaotic. Rather, the movement of God's Spirit keeps in rhythm with the Father's and Son's heart.

On the Day of Pentecost, the Spirit broke in like a rushing wind and caused all the disciples to speak in other languages. It was something that took the disciples by surprise. The Scriptures repeatedly point to the Spirit of the Father and the Son as living and active. Accordingly, the Spirit of God is compared to a river, fire, and wind.[35] Like these elements, God moves with great force, spontaneity, and steadiness.

Think of people who have lots of energy and passion. One such person was the famous singer and dancer, James Brown. You might say that the Spirit is like him, only more intense! Full of joy and excitement. The Holy Spirit of the Father and the Son has the most energy out of any person in the universe. He is invisible, but for those with eyes to see and ears to hear, He is loud, wild, and free.

And the same goes for Jesus. One of the more memorable moments of the Old Testament was when David wildly danced before the Lord (see 2 Samuel 6:14). David was a prophetic shadow of the Messiah to come. In fact, Jesus was called the "son of David," which was a term used to describe the Christ. If David (who was merely a shadow of the Messiah to come) danced extravagantly before the Lord, how much more does the actual Messiah, the Son of God, dance before His Father!

---

35. Here are some of the Scriptures where the Spirit of God is compared to these things: Psalm 36:8; John 3:8; Hebrews 12:29.

THE HAPPY TRINITY

Psalm 149 tells the children of God to "dance" to the Lord. Now think about this. The goal of all God's commands is that we would be Christ-like. We are ultimately being called and conformed to the glorious image of Christ Himself. So, if God tells His people to dance, it's because His Son, Christ, must also dance!

The dance of the Trinity is simple. It's the movement of love from the Father to the Son and the Son to the Father. They love each other, rejoice in each other, and sing to one another. Zephaniah 3 shows that the Lord sings 1and dances (exults) over His people with joy. And He invites His people into this same dance today!

Chapter Five: The Wrath of the Trinity

> *"So I am eager to preach the gospel to*
> *you also who are in Rome... For the wrath*
> *of God is revealed from heaven..."*
> Romans 1:15, 18

Paul's letter to the Romans has always been known as one of the main books that unpacks the gospel. It is filled with the *good news* of Christ's death and resurrection and what that means for the world. In the very first chapter, Paul introduces his audience to the *wrath of God*. So how does the wrath of the Trinity fit in with "good news?"

We must learn through the Scriptures that God's wrath is not at odds with His joy. The Father, Son, and Spirit are united and Their love, joy, and wrath work together for our good. Let's look at this a little bit more.

The Gospel of Wrath

The Greek word for "wrath" has an interesting meaning. The most basic definition is "desire." Yes, there is an "anger" in God's wrath, but there is more to the word than just anger. The Greek word for wrath is *orge*. In simple terms, it means "intense desire or passion."[36]

The word paints a picture of an *intense desire that leads to wild passion*.[37] In the first century, Paul's audience would not have associated "wrath" with anger only, but also with *intense passion*. Was the word still intimidating? Yes. But it also wasn't a reason to discard God's love. God's love and God's wrath went hand in hand.

Paul is crazy enough to say that in the good news of the Gospel, "The wrath of God is revealed from heaven against all ungodliness and unrighteousness of men, who by their unrighteousness suppress the truth" (Romans 1:18). Here's the thing: The wrath of God *is* good news. Ungodliness and unrighteousness need to be dealt with. The torment, the pain, the lies of the enemy, sin, the lust of the flesh, and the pride of life are all things that do damage to human beings. And so, God sent His Son into the world to destroy the works of darkness (see 1 John 3:8).

---

36. "Lexicon: Strong's G3709: *Orge*" (https://www.blueletterbible.org/lang/lexicon/lexicon.cfm?Strongs=G3709&t=KJV).

37. "Orge" is where we get the English word "orgy." The English word "orgy" is defined by the Google Dictionary as "an instance of excessive indulgence in a specified activity" (www.google.com/dictionary). You can see here the wild passion and intensity associated with this word.

CHAPTER FIVE: THE WRATH OF THE TRINITY

It is vital that we see that God's passionate wrath is *for us*. If God were a lazy and indifferent Father, He would have left us in our sin. But God is a *good Father*. He didn't leave us in darkness. Instead, the gospel reveals the wrath and passion of our Father from heaven. This is good news!

The wrath of the Father, the Son, and the Spirit is the violent passion to destroy the works of the devil in order to set us free! Sin entered the world through Adam and Eve and God's passion was aroused. He would not sit back and let His kids be tormented. He has way too much glorious energy to not do anything. Therefore, in His wrath, God prepared a way to destroy sin.

Old Testament Wrath

God's wrath was stirred up from the beginning. It began with Adam and Eve as they "exchanged the truth about God for a lie" (Romans 1:25). God created humans to live in the truth of God as their Father, the Son as their Life, and the Spirit as their Helper. Instead, humans turned to idols. They worshipped and served created things instead of the Creator. Sin then arose out of the lies that we believed. This led to deeds of unrighteousness.

The whole thing was a lie from the devil to begin with. Adam and Eve were created in the "likeness" of God. The devil told Eve that if she ate of the apple she would be "like" God (Genesis 3:5). And yet, they were *already created* in the "likeness" of their Creator. It was a deception that made humanity question the gift of the Father.

THE HAPPY TRINITY

God had always given us more than enough. His own breath of life was within us from the very beginning. But when we fell for the lie, we fell into sin and death as well! And God's wrath and passion were aroused. He was not okay with letting His children be lost forever. He sought out Adam, asking him, "Where are you?" (Genesis 3:9) It was then that God, in His passionate love, promised to one day destroy the work of the devil. He told the serpent that Eve's offspring would soon "bruise your head" (Genesis 3:15).

The story of God's passion for us would continue with the prophets. They also testified to the wrath of God. Isaiah, Jeremiah, Ezekiel, and others all told their audiences of the wrath of God against sin. God never let up in His pursuit of us. He wasn't "okay" with us living under slavery to wickedness.

Are you beginning to see that the wrath of God has a purpose? It's not wrath for the sake of wrath. God's wrath has been leading us somewhere all along. It has been leading us back to His joy.

Earlier we looked at Jeremiah 32, which is quite an illuminating passage. There you find that God brings His wrath against His people, because they were sacrificing their children to a false god (Jeremiah 32:35). Let's stop right there for a moment: Isn't it good news that we have a God who is *against* the murder of innocent children? It's good to know that His wrath is perfect. Remember, this is a God who existed in an *intimate relationship of perfect love, joy, laughter, and freedom* before the world began. The Trinity created these incredible creatures who

CHAPTER FIVE: THE WRATH OF THE TRINITY

bore Their image. *And then the creation started killing its own children!* Of course, the Trinity would not be happy about this!

It is really out of God's kindness that He shows wrath against this kind of behavior! After Jeremiah preached on God's wrath due to child sacrifice, he then revealed God's true desire for the people:

> *"I will make with them an everlasting covenant, that I will not turn away from doing good to them…I will rejoice in doing them good, and I will plant them in this land in faithfulness, with all My heart and all my soul."*
> (Jeremiah 32:40-41)

Jeremiah told them that God would, "Rejoice in doing them good with all of His heart and all of His soul." *That's the heart of God throughout the whole Bible and throughout all of history.* Through all of the wrath, God's heart never changed. His wrath and passion was, and remains, congruent with His desire to rejoice in His people. His wrath protects and saves His people from destroying themselves (literally killing their own children).

The Jews may not have understood this at the time, but God's wrath against their sin was the same thing as His joy over them. His abundant joy could not and would not let them continue to kill their children. In other words, their sin was killing the joy God had created for them in the first place. He just wanted them to live in His glorious blessing.

When you think of any judgments of wrath in the Old Testament, keep this in mind: God's goal was always to rejoice over His people with gladness and singing (Zephaniah 3:17). His wrath is intense and passionate discipline that leads to joy. He is a good Father with wrath and passion towards anything that stops His children from joining in with this eternal joy.

The Wrath of the Lamb

The theme of God's wrath that disciplines us for our ultimate good is true throughout all of Scripture. Isaiah said that when God judges, the world learns righteousness (Isaiah 26:9). His judgments are *good*. They are fully in line with His overwhelming joy over humanity. And all of this wrath is leading to the most hilarious thing: "Let the earth rejoice; let all of the islands be glad" (Psalm 97:1)! His wrath is making all things new and wiping away every tear in this world!

The book of Revelation has a funny and ironic phrase: *The wrath of the Lamb* (Revelation 6:16). Think about that phrase for a moment. A lamb isn't exactly a violent or terrifying creature. Yet the phrase makes sense when we realize that the Lamb in the book of Revelation is the same Lamb who gave His life for the whole world. His "wrath" guides the earth into its glorious destiny of joy, peace, and love. This kind of wrath is rooted in the tender mercies of God's lamb-like heart. First century listeners would have found this phrase—the wrath of the Lamb—incredibly comforting in comparison to the wrath of the Roman

CHAPTER FIVE: THE WRATH OF THE TRINITY

Emperors. In their wrath, such kings would torture and crucify people all throughout the world. But in a refreshing contrast, the Lamb of God, the King of all kings, would lay down His life down for His people.

It's *this* Lamb that all the Old Testament prophets were pointing to. Jesus walked with His disciples on the road to Emmaus and showed them how the law and the prophets were always pointing to His sufferings and resurrection (Luke 24:27). Likewise, Peter said that the prophets all told of the grace and glory that was to come through the sufferings of Christ (1 Peter 1:10-11).

The greatest display of God's wrath was at the cross.[38] It was there that He poured out all of His "violent passion" onto sin. All of that passion led Christ to take the entirety of the world's sin onto Himself (John 1:29). He took it all into His grave and buried it forever. The Father, Son, and Spirit were united at the cross. It wasn't only the Father's wrath, but the Son's and the Spirit's as well. All three Persons of the Trinity wanted to destroy sin and death and, through Christ's death and resurrection, that's exactly what They did. Now, we access it through faith.

The wrath of God is truly good news. We were enslaved to sin, and if God didn't have wrath against sin, we would be enslaved to it forever. The Father, because of His wrath, sent His Son to the cross to free us from slavery. It is in the work of the cross that we place our faith—a faith

---

[38]. A quick note on "future wrath" (1 Thessalonians 1:10). For those who persist in sin and a refusal of the gift of the gospel, there will always be a place of wrath that comes from the loving heart of the Father.

THE HAPPY TRINITY

that realizes that Christ did not die alone. *Our corrupt and sinful nature died with Christ!* (Romans 6:6 & Galatians 2:20). The Trinity's wrath crucified and buried our sinful nature. It is completely through the Father's wrath (and His passionate joy and love), displayed through the work of Christ, that we are made brand new. When we receive this by faith, a fountain of joy, peace, and hope opens up within us.

So, let's make this totally clear: The wrath of the Trinity is one and the same with His love and joy. His love and joy were not satisfied to leave His children imprisoned. There is no difference between the overwhelming happiness of God and His intense and fiery wrath. At the cross, the Father's infinite gladness over His kids erupted into a violent passion against sin, forever setting us free. Praise the Father, Son, and Spirit for the work of Their divine wrath on the cross!

Chapter Six: The Grace of the Trinity

"Grace to you and peace from God our Father and the Lord Jesus Christ."
Ephesians 1:2

Let's talk about the "grace" of the Trinity. Grace is an extremely common word in Christianity and it gets tossed around a lot. We know for sure that the gospel is a "gospel of grace" (Acts 20:24). Paul frequently uses the term "grace" in his letters to describe what God has done through Christ. He even opens up his letters with grace and peace from God our Father. What then, does the "grace of God" really mean?

When Powerful Words Grow Stale

Over time, certain words lose their power. The word "grace" in the first century caused an explosion of love, joy, and peace, which the world hadn't seen before. The word "grace" in the first century was a Greek word called *charis*. This was a commonly used word that simply meant "kindness."[39] Multitudes of people in the first century came to a realization that the Creator of the universe was *kind!* This shook the culture to its core!

Think about how even today there is this subtle (yet not so subtle) belief that God is angry with the world. If not angry, certainly at least disappointed! And if not disappointed, certainly He is distant and doesn't really care. Oh, how far this is from the original truth of Christ and His world-changing message!

When you look in a Greek Bible dictionary and find the word "grace," you will see two things: The first thing you find is what the word actually meant to the people of the first century, which was good-will, loving-kindness, and favor. But then you get a nice definition that scholars have put together, which is usually what translates into sermons and the general panorama of Christian thought throughout the world. It's usually something like this:

"Grace is the merciful kindness of God exerting His holy influence upon souls, turning them to Christ, keeping them, strengthening them, and increasing them in the Christian faith."[40]

Now hear me out. That is a great definition and *I appreciate it*. But here's the thing: While that definition might be theologically correct, it's not really what the original audience was thinking when they heard the word "grace."

---

39. "Lexicon: Strong's G5485: Charis" (https://www.blueletterbible.org/lang/lexicon/lexicon.cfm?Strongs=G5485&t=KJV).
40. Ibid.

CHAPTER SIX: THE GRACE OF THE TRINITY

In the first century, "grace" was simply a common word associated with kindness and sweetness. It was a word that everybody valued and used for people or things that were actually *delightful, beautiful, nice, tasty, sweet, and kind*. It wasn't a fancy word that only church people used. It was a universal word about something amazingly kind, and people discovered that they could use it to describe the God and Father of the Lord Jesus Christ!

Grace is the Overflow of God's Joy!

Allow me to drop one more bomb on you. The Greek word for grace was a word that came from another root word known as *chairo*. It's important to understand the root word because the first century hearers of the gospel would have definitely associated the word "grace" with its root word. The words were very close, like a big brother to a little brother. What then did the root word *chairo* mean?

Well, this might offend some grumpy Pharisees out there, but the word *chairo* meant "to rejoice exceedingly, to be cheerful or happy."[41] This was a common word to describe someone who was very happy! Not "kind-of-happy," but *exceedingly happy*.

Joy was the root of grace!

The first century listeners of the gospel would hear that God is a God of *grace* and would instantly understand that

---

41. "Lexicon: Strong's G5463: Chairo" (https://www.blueletterbible.org/lang/lexicon/lexicon.cfm?strongs=G5463&t=KJV).

THE HAPPY TRINITY

He is a God who is exceedingly joyful. People understood that the God of "grace" had a smile on His face!

It was this discovery of God's gracious and joyful heart that caused all the commotion in the book of Acts. This is what "turned the world upside down" (Acts 17:6). It was a whole bunch of people who believed that the living God was exceedingly happy, kind, and sweet. It was a complete disruption to all the religions, cultures, politics, and systems that ran off of fear and control.

The apostles were calling the world to repent from their sin and trust in a rejoicing God who had shown the world His magnificent *grace*. They were sharing the greatest news to ever hit planet earth. Some thought the apostles were absolutely crazy and should be either be imprisoned or killed. Many of them were killed! But despite the risk, the apostles continued to proclaim this revolutionary message.

To put it simply one more time: God's "grace" is His overwhelming happiness overflowing into kindness towards His creation. Just as *chairo* is the root word for *charis*, the joy of God is the root and foundation of His kind and saving actions toward us. This was how the simple Greeks and Jews heard these things when the gospel was first announced. These are the word associations they made in their heads. The prophet Micah said it well, that God "delights in mercy" (Micah 7:18 NKJV). God's mercy doesn't just *happen*; it comes out of His joy and delight.

Think about it like this: Does someone who is filled with anger naturally show kindness? Absolutely not. People who are generally happy with themselves and with

CHAPTER SIX: THE GRACE OF THE TRINITY

life are more likely to be kind to others. In the same way, God's grace and kindness came flowing out of His eternal happiness and joy.

From Jesus, We Received Grace Upon Grace

All of these wonderful characteristics of God's joy and kindness are what led to the death and resurrection of Christ. It's not like God is this amazing Happy Trinity who left us here to figure out life on our own. He actually did something to eternally rescue us. It was God's happy grace that sent His Son to the cross to bear our sin and secure our place in His family forever.

As we discussed previously, God's wrath was against the sin that enslaved us. His grace and wrath worked together at the cross to condemn and judge sin itself. Jesus took our sin upon Himself so that we could actually step out of it and be free. (2 Corinthians 5:21) The Father and Son were united in Their grace and wrath, which would absolutely destroy sin and bring us into true liberty.

It was because "God so loved the world" that He sent Jesus to the cross. It's God's *sweet kindness*—not fear—that leads humanity to repentance (see 1 John 4:18 & Romans 2:4). God's loving-kindness destroyed sin for us in the Person of His Son. This is the revelation that set the world on fire and upset the Roman Empire and led to great persecution. When the happy and kind God is preached, people can sometimes get their heads cut off (like the apostle Paul for example). Emperors and religious leaders do not always like the message of a happy God. Jesus preached about His gloriously good Father and got killed as well. So, let's not be surprised if this message doesn't always "sit well" with others.

When the good news of God's great joy begins to set people free, it can really shake things up and upset the status quo. Yet this is at the heart of why Christ came to the earth. He came here to "make the Father known" (John 17:26). The pinnacle of this mission was revealed at the cross, where we were clearly shown what the living God is like. The cross revealed the unconditional love of the Father for the whole world. As humanity killed God's own Son, the Son said, "Father, forgive them"—and He did. The living Trinity of sweet love and dancing joy had shown the entire universe that They are overwhelmingly kind, in spite of humanity's wickedness.

Much of the New Testament letters written to new or growing believers begin with an important blessing of "grace and peace" from God the Father and the Lord Jesus Christ. Today, let's return to the original joy of this statement. Let's get beyond the stale images that are commonplace in our minds and see what the first century audience saw:

Grace and peace from God our Father and the Lord Jesus Christ. Grace ... kindness ... sweetness ... exceeding happiness ... from the living God ... the Creator of the universe ... Who forgave all my sins ... and gave me new life through His Son's blood ...

Chapter Seven: The Gospel of the Trinity

"That the world may know that You sent Me and loved them even as You loved Me."
John 17:23

There has been a lot of good news in this book so far, but this chapter reveals perhaps the most stunning truth of all—that we have been decisively included in the *relationship of the Trinity*. But before we go further into this and unpack its riches, first we must understand why we were originally created.

The Original Blessing

There is an "original blessing" that God placed upon us. In the beginning, Adam and Eve were created as a son and daughter of God. In the New Testament, Luke states this clearly when he writes that Adam was a "son of God" (Luke 3:38). On top of this, Adam and Eve are also described as being created in the "image of God"

(Genesis 1:26). The terms "son" and "image" are central to the identity and purpose of humanity and they connect powerfully with Christ.

Remember that Christ is the *eternal Son and the true image of God.* As Paul wrote to the Colossians, Christ is "the image of the invisible God" (Colossians 1:15). This shows us that from the beginning, Adam and Eve were created to be sons, daughters, and images of God just like Jesus was the eternal Son and image of God. He is the original Child of the Father, but the Father wanted to create more children—and that is how we got here. We are the younger brothers and sisters of Christ (Hebrews 2:12)!

It's like the apostle John said: "As He is so also are we" (1 John 4:17). Our original purpose for being created was to be just like the Son of God. We were created to be "co-heirs" with Christ (Romans 8:17). This means that we were created to be loved by the Father, just like Christ. Out of this love, we were also made to share in Christ's joy simply by being the sons and daughters of God.

Restoration!

The gospel can be understood as a gospel of "restoration." The apostle Peter said that God is restoring all things (Acts 3:21). But what does this restoration look like? It is humanity living as the children of God we were always created to be. "Reconciling all things back to Himself" is about humanity being restored to the way things were meant to be—restored to the original blessing of our Father (see Colossians 1:20).

CHAPTER SEVEN: THE GOSPEL OF THE TRINITY

Every human being is a unique expression and image of God. All of us are one-of-a-kind sons or daughters, held together by Christ Himself (Colossians 1:16-17). In Jesus's teachings, He often went out of His way to say that even the "outcasts"—the poor, the lepers, the prostitutes—were valuable to the Father (see Luke 15:1).

Even after the fall of man, God showed His heart to Abraham, the father of the Jewish people, when He promised that through Abraham's seed (Christ), all the families of the earth would be blessed (Genesis 12:3). God's heart was always for the world to be restored and reconciled to the Father.

We became blind to God, twisted in our thinking, and corrupt in our hearts (Colossians 1:21). But God always remained good, happy, and joyful in the relationship of the Trinity. The good news is that He didn't leave us stuck in our condition, but He sent His Son to do something about our fallen state. In His great mercy and gentleness, the Son entered our sinful condition to completely deliver us out of it. God's joy over us led Him to crucify our sinful nature to the cross and restore us to the original blessing of being sons and daughters of the Father, in fellowship with the Son and Spirit.

Paul tells us 81 different times in the New Testament that we are "in Christ." This means that we are *one with Christ.* Marriage is a symbol of this divine mystery (Ephesians 5:22-33). Paul wrote to the Corinthians, "'The two will become one flesh.' But he who is joined to the Lord is one with Him in spirit" (1 Corinthians 6:16-17).

We are one with the Eternal Son of God and therefore have entered into the relationship of the Happy Trinity.

Entering the Son's Relationship with the Father

Here's something funny about the gospel: We don't get to have our own difficult relationship with the Father. We get to have a relationship through the *Son's relationship with the Father.* In other words, we don't get to have some grueling "valley to mountaintop to valley to mountaintop to valley to mountaintop" relationship with God. It may sound odd, but the good news is that we get to enter into the Son's perfect relationship with the Father. That's what it means to be "in Christ."

Let's unpack this a little bit. Through the work of Christ, we have received the "Spirit of the Son" by which we cry "Abba, Father!" (Galatians 4:6) Christ Himself, the Son of God, lives in us and we live in Him. Our relationship with the Father is through the Son. This is what Paul means when he says those 81 times that we are "in Christ." The Father relates to us based on this reality. *He deals with us the same way He deals with Christ.*

The Father spoke from heaven towards Jesus, "This is my Beloved Son with whom I am well pleased" (Matthew 3:17). And now, since you are in Jesus, He says the same thing over you. This just might be the greatest revelation of the gospel. The same way the Father loves the Son, with all infinite happiness and joy, He loves you! Not because

CHAPTER SEVEN: THE GOSPEL OF THE TRINITY

of anything you did; rather, it's just by virtue of you being *in Christ*. It's not by works but by grace through simply believing it (faith!).

Everything we have discovered about the Trinity has been leading to this. The happiness, the laughter, the dancing, and the love with which the Father loves the Son—also comes from the Father, *toward you.* This is the gospel!

And what if I told you that this is the very thing Jesus Himself prayed for. He prayed to the Father, "That the world may know that You sent Me and *have loved them even as You loved Me*" (John 17:23).

Take a deep breath and receive this glorious gospel into your heart. The Father loves you in the same way He loves the Son.

In the next verse, Jesus reminds the Father, "You loved Me before the foundation of the world" (John 17:24). The absolutely incredible, out-of-this-world love with which the Father loved the Son before the earth began is also directed *at us.* The happiness, joy, laughter, playfulness, delight, and infinite love that the Father has always had for His perfect one and only Son, He also has for us. The way He played and laughed with His Son when He made the world (Proverbs 8:30-31) is the same way He laughs and plays with you now as He re-creates this world.

And that same joy that the Son of God has eternally existed in, is now ours. Jesus prayed to the Father, "I say these things while I am still in the world, so that they may have the full measure of My joy within them" (John 17:13). The eternal Son of God laid down His life for us so that we can share in the same joy that He has always had in His Father's love. We too have been anointed with the oil of gladness by the delight of the Father (Hebrews 1:9).

As quoted earlier, Charles Spurgeon said, "The joy of Jesus is, first, the joy of abiding in His Father's love. He knows that His Father loves Him… That is the joy which Christ gives to you— the joy of knowing that your Father loves you…even as Jesus Christ is loved."[42]

It is the joy of being loved that is ours in Christ. Nothing can separate us from His love (Romans 8:38-39.) Victor Hugo, the author of the classic book *Les Misérables,* wrote, "The supreme happiness of life consists in the conviction that one is loved."[43] The ultimate happiness of both Jesus and us is that we are loved by the Father with a perfect love that casts out all fear.

This is the mission of the Son—to reveal to us the Father's love and to share His joy with us. After He rose from the dead, Jesus appeared to Mary Magdalene and said, "Go instead to My brothers and tell them, 'I am returning to My Father and your Father, to My God and your God'" (John 20:17). Jesus is communicating that His victory over sin and death restores us to our original blessing of being sons and daughters of God, which also means being the little brothers and sisters of Jesus! He tells us that His Father is our Father and that His Father loves us

---
42. Charles H. Spurgeon, "Christ's Joy and Ours" (Sermon #2935).
43. Hugo, *Les Misérables*, Ch. 4.

CHAPTER SEVEN: THE GOSPEL OF THE TRINITY

and delights in us the same way He loves and delights in Him. We are in Christ. Never forget it.

What C.S. Lewis wrote is our truest reality and we can identify with it completely: "The Happy Trinity is her home: nothing can trouble her joy. She is the bird that evades every net: the wild deer that leaps every pitfall. Like the mother bird to its chickens or a shield to the armed knight: so is the Lord to her mind, in His unchanging lucidity."[44] In the Son by the Spirit, loved by the Father; we are home in the Happy Trinity.

---

44. Lewis, The Great Divorce, 134.

Chapter Eight: The Drink of the Trinity

> *"The Gospel is like wine which makes us glad."*
> Charles Spurgeon

Jesus used wine to symbolize His blood poured out for the world—blood that was shed to bring humanity back into the original blessing of the Father's joy. This wine of the New Covenant between God and man is the greatest drink in the universe. It is spiritual wine. It is the good news that God has poured out his Son on the cross in order to save us.

The wine of His blood is a drink that produces true spiritual joy. Just like regular wine takes away people's worries and helps them to loosen up, the wine of Jesus does it all the more. The good news that Jesus has taken away all our sins, anxieties, and worries is like wine to our hearts. We are called to continually drink of this New Covenant wine! Perhaps this is why Jesus's first miracle was to turn water into wine (John 2).

THE HAPPY TRINITY

Charles Spurgeon had some beautiful thoughts on this subject. He said, "The Gospel is like wine which makes us glad. Let a man truly know the Grace of our Lord Jesus Christ, and he will be a happy man! And the deeper he drinks into the Spirit of Christ, the more happy will he become!"[45]

The Drink of Heaven

Drinking down the good news is the solution to alcoholism and every kind of addiction. People get addicted to alcohol, drugs, pornography and sex because of the pleasure derived from these things. The hearts of men and women were created by God to experience pleasure (Psalm 16:11). We're thirsty for it and won't settle for a life without it.

Thankfully, the prophet Isaiah declared that the true wine from above would be freely given to us by God: "Come, everyone who thirsts, come to the waters; and he who has no money, come, buy and eat! Come buy wine and milk without money and without price" (Isaiah 55:1-2).

All around the world people are spending billions of dollars on drugs, alcohol, and sex and they still aren't satisfied. Meanwhile, God is saying, "Come to Me and you can have My wine for free!" We were created for happiness and to delight in God and all of life. It is through opening our hearts to His drink of His spiritual wine that our inner senses awaken, and we can experience joy everlasting.

---

45. Charles H. Spurgeon, "A Free Salvation" (Sermon #199).

CHAPTER EIGHT: THE DRINK OF THE TRINITY

Proverbs 9 says that the Wisdom of God has made mixed wine for us to drink. As we saw earlier, Paul explained to the Corinthians that Christ *is* the wisdom of God (1 Corinthians 1:30). Christ's love is like the intense mixed wine of Proverbs. And we are being *wise* when we receive it into our lives!

In *The Great Divorce* by C.S. Lewis, one character asks the Spirit, "Why do I exist?" And the Spirit responds, "For infinite happiness…you can step out into it at any moment."[46] The Infinite Happiness is God Himself and He offers Himself freely to all people at all times. Those who seek, find.

Jesus repeated Isaiah's prophecy and pointed to Himself as the ultimate thirst-quencher. He stood up and said, "If anyone thirsts, let him come to Me and drink. Whoever believes in Me, as the Scripture has said, 'Out of his heart will flow rivers of living water'" (John 7:37-38). There is a living drink that Jesus offers to us daily. It quenches the deepest thirst of our beings. When we learn to drink from it, we are freed from our addictions, which turn out to be "lesser pleasures," "softer drinks," and "inadequate highs."

Paul made the same connection when he told the church in Ephesus to not get drunk with wine, but instead be filled with the Spirit (Ephesians 5:18). He was saying that the Spirit is the *true wine and the true drink* that satisfies more than any earthly liquor.

As we continue to discover that God is a Happy Trinity, we grow in our relationship with Him. We accept that He

---

46. Lewis, The Great Divorce, 61.

Himself *is* the drink. By faith, we receive His Spirit and allow His love to fill our hearts. This spiritual drink then fills our lives with more and more love, joy, and peace—all of which has been fully given to us through Christ's death and resurrection. In Christ, we have been given an unending supply of spiritual wine. Indeed, we are given the complete fullness of God Himself! (Colossians 2:9-10)

At the very end of the Bible, there is a yet another invitation to come and drink, revealing how central and important this issue really is. "Whoever is thirsty," Jesus shouts, "let him come; and whoever wishes, let him take the free gift of the water of life" (Revelation 22:17). This spiritual drink of love and joy is freely offered to everybody everywhere! Let *anyone* who is thirsty for happiness drink freely from the Father's love in Jesus.

This pleasure of drinking in God's love is what we were created for in the beginning when we were placed in the Garden of Pleasure. What we lost in the fall has been restored in Christ. Now we are free to once again experience all the pleasures that exist within God. As the Psalmist wrote, "In Your presence there is fullness of joy; at Your right hand there are pleasures forevermore" (Psalm 16:11).

The Call to Ecstasy

Drug addicts get looked down upon like they are worse than the rest. But the truth is, they are often more honest than the rest. We were created to be happy in God. We weren't made for a dull life without any inner exhilaration

CHAPTER EIGHT: THE DRINK OF THE TRINITY

or wonder. Drug addicts seek to get high and alcoholics seek to get drunk because they know we were created for more than just "normal life." The problem is that they are looking for these things in the wrong places. They are missing the real heavenly substance for which we were made. A substance that produces spiritual ecstasy.

It's interesting to discover that the term "ecstasy" was originally a biblical word and its purpose was to describe experiences with God.[47] The New Testament uses this Greek term over 20 times.[48] It shows us that we were created for spiritual "ecstasies" with the Father. We were made to encounter His love and to be filled with amazement and astonishment. When we experience His presence, we are often filled with wonder.

The word "ecstasy" means to "stand outside oneself." Edith Humphrey, a New Testament Professor at Pittsburgh Theological Seminary, gives a great explanation of it. Regarding the term's biblical context, she writes this about ecstasy: "It thus refers to the abandonment of self as one goes out to the other. It is that ecstatic movement, which it seems, enables the mysterious intimacy between the Divine Persons."[49]

---

47. Benjamin Dunn, *The Happy Gospel!: Effortless Union with a Happy God,* (Shippensburg, PA: Destiny Image Publishers Inc., 2011), 49.

48. "Lexicon: Strong's G1611: Ekstasis" (https://www.blueletterbible.org/lang/lexicon/lexicon.cfm?Strongs=G1611&t=KJV). And "Lexicon: Strong's G1839: Existemi" (Available online at https://www.blueletterbible.org/lang/lexicon/lexicon.cfm?strongs=G1839&t=KJV).

49. Edith M. Humphry, *Ecstasy and Intimacy: When the Holy Spirit Meets the Human Spirit,* (Grand Rapids, MI: Wm. B. Eerdmans Publishing Co., 2006), 4.

Humphrey goes on to say that "as Christians, we celebrate and proclaim the 'ecstasy' of God the Son, His going out to us, and standing with us. The good news is that God Himself has visited us. Jesus, our Lord, has been baptized into the deepest elements of our world, has lived our life perfectly, has died our death righteously, has conquered that death in resurrection, and has ascended to the Father, taking up human flesh in triumph and glory."[50]

At times, spiritual "ecstasies" provide supernatural visions and images within a person, all of which are meant to produce purity, love, and inexpressible joy. "Your sons and your daughters shall prophesy, and your young men shall see visions," the prophet Joel said (Joel 2:28). Jesus's ecstasy becomes ours through our oneness with Him. Like Christ, we now pour *our lives* out to the world as we "stand outside ourselves" in ecstasy.

The Scriptures teach that both Peter and Paul experienced "ecstasies" with God. Acts 10:10 says this about Peter: "And he became hungry and desired to eat. But as they were making ready an ecstasy came upon him." Then, Acts 22:17 tells us this about Paul's encounter: "And it came to pass when I had returned to Jerusalem, and as I was praying in the temple, that I became in ecstasy."[51]

People idolize the pleasures of alcohol, drugs, and sex, but fail to fill the void within them and satisfy their deepest

---

50. Edith M. Humphry, *Ecstasy and Intimacy: When the Holy Spirit Meets the Human Spirit,* (Grand Rapids, MI: Wm. B. Eerdmans Publishing Co., 2006), 4.

51. *The Holy Scriptures,* (British & Foreign Bible Society, 1890, 2012) John Nelson Darby.

CHAPTER EIGHT: THE DRINK OF THE TRINITY

cravings. Our hearts long for something more and thus we become satisfied when we drink in the love of God.

The ecstasy that Jesus provides makes us more happy, whole, and pure than any drug this world offers. It is the greatest wine—sweet to the taste and intoxicating to the soul. Our minds finally come to rest when we receive the love of the Most High God. God heightens our spiritual senses and gives us more peace than a gram of heroin ever could. His Spirit gives us more wholeness than any hit of crystal meth. We were created for peace, joy, and wonder, and drugs cannot give them to us. Only God can.

Experiencing God

The Gospel leaves us with one option: to partake, receive, drink, and eat! It's time to open wide and drink in the everlasting waters of His gladness. David said that we are to "drink from the river of God's pleasures" (Psalm 36:8). Randy Alcorn wrote that the "wonderful responsibility" of the gospel is "like being required to eat Mom's apple pie!"[52] We must feast!

The reason many people struggle to experience God is because they are looking for a God who is distant, boring, lifeless, aloof, silent, and completely focused on moral failures. The funny thing is, this God does not exist! This is not what the real God is like! So, if you're looking for the God who is keeping track of your sins up in the sky,

---

52. Alcorn, Happiness, 18.

you're certainly going to struggle to experience "Him." That's a non-god!

Now on the other hand, the living and *real* God is filled with infinite energy. He has more energy than a million kids with ADHD. He is more active than we can comprehend. As we've seen before, this God is playing and laughing all around us in billions of ways. He is literally holding every little thing together right at this moment (Colossians 1:17). And He doesn't hold everything together begrudgingly. He is rejoicing to sustain all things. As we read earlier, the psalmist declared, "Praise God forever! How He must rejoice in all His work!" (Psalm 104:31 TLB)

When we begin to look for the Father who Jesus reveals—the God who is anointed with the oil of gladness above all His companions (Hebrews 1:9), the God who rejoices with his friends when His children return home (Luke 15), the God who prays for His joy to be made complete in us (John 17:13)—we begin to find Him very easily. He is not far. He is in us, with us, and in everyone and everything around us.

We also tend to rely on our own minds when trying to experience God. We think that we will only experience God once all of the thoughts in our head line up in some perfectly logical way—like God is some math equation that we need to figure out. But God's peace and His happy presence are experienced beyond our understanding. "You will experience God's peace, which is far more wonderful than the human mind can understand" (Philippians 4:7 TLB).

CHAPTER EIGHT: THE DRINK OF THE TRINITY

Joy is the frequency of what it's like to experience God. When we simply look for the God whose very presence is joy, we begin to discover the rhythm of joy. Experiencing God is often more like listening to music, or dancing with a partner, than having an intellectual conversation with a philosopher. His presence is easy and light (Matthew 11:29). Experiencing Him is like drinking from a river (Psalm 36:8), feeling the wind (John 3:8), or drinking wine (Proverbs 9:2-5). Being "filled with the Spirit" is like music, water, wine, or wind filling your entire being, silencing all of your fears and anxieties. His peace is tangible and can be felt just like anxiety can be felt. *But His peace is way more powerful.* Above all, He is a Family, Father, Brother and Comforter that wants you to feel at home in Him.

Brother Lawrence

Brother Lawrence became famous for just being an ordinary guy who was aware that God was always with him. His few letters to a friend, a friend that he specifically asked not to turn into a book, were published as *The Practice of the Presence of God*. Fortunately to this day, it remains a foundational classic on how to experience and grow in relationship with God.

In this book Brother Lawrence tells his friend how he lived his life, day to day, with a simple awareness of God's love. He was nobody special at all. He had no unique superpowers other than being an ordinary human being who worked as a cook. Yet people would come from miles away to speak with him and to even watch him

THE HAPPY TRINITY

cook, just because there was a presence about him that was contagious!

Brother Lawrence wrote in his letter, "I make it my business only to persevere in His holy presence, wherein I keep myself by a simple attention, and a general fond regard to God, which I may call an actual *presence* of God; or, to speak better, an habitual, silent, and secret conversation of the soul with God, which often causes me joys and raptures inwardly, and sometimes also outwardly, so great that I am forced to use means to moderate them and prevent their appearance to others."[53]

Lawrence stated in another letter, "I cannot imagine how religious persons can live satisfied without the practice of the presence of God."[54] This shows us that it's not good just to be a religious person by name. If that's all religion is, then everyone is better off ditching religion. The teachings of Brother Lawrence, however, remind us that there is a real tangible presence that makes the gospel message the most powerful thing in the world: God is really at work in our lives and He is a real presence—a real Person.

Being aware of His presence is not hard at all. Think about Christ. Is it hard for Him to experience the Father? No! There's no striving in His presence. His yoke is easy and His burden is light. It's easier than breathing air. You don't "think" your way into it. Your heart and mind simply

---

53. Brother Lawrence, *The Practice of the Presence of God*, (Old Tappan, NJ: Fleming H. Revel Company, 1958), 36.
54. Lawrence, The Practice of the Presence of God, 46.

CHAPTER EIGHT: THE DRINK OF THE TRINITY

become aware of the One who is already here, there, and everywhere!

Lawrence continued, "He requires no great matters of us. You need not cry very loud; He is nearer to us than we are aware of."[55] The truth is, God has been speaking to all of us, all along. He has never *not* been around us. He's God and His love is everywhere! The universe exists *in Him.* We've all been experiencing God our whole lives, it's time to just wake up and realize it. This is what "repentance" is all about. God is all around us and He is not going anywhere. The fullness of His joy fills the earth. So, it's time to repent and turn to this glorious God!

Lawrence said, "Everyone is capable of such familiar conversation with God."[56] This echoes a prophecy from Jeremiah which is for us today: "No longer will a man teach his neighbor, or a man his brother, saying, 'Know the Lord,' because they will all know Me, from the least of them to the greatest, for I will forgive their wickedness and will remember their sins no more" (Jeremiah 31:34). This is clearly a New Covenant promise that we can all know God for ourselves.

When we give our simple attention to the God who *is love,* we are met by the pure affection of our Father. He surrounds us in every way. Lawrence wrote, "The King, full of mercy and goodness, very far from chastising me, embraces me with love, makes me eat at His table, serves me with His own hands, gives me the key of His treasures;

---
55. Lawrence, The Practice of the Presence of God, 48.
56. Ibid, 49.

THE HAPPY TRINITY

He converses and delights Himself with me incessantly, in a thousand and a thousand ways, and treats me in all respects as His favorite. It is thus I consider myself from time to time in His holy presence."[57]

A happy life can be found in the simple awareness of God's love. Brother Lawrence taught us that experiencing God is not hard and it's not for the spiritually elite. Moreover, we can experience God in the regular spaces of day to day life. Whether we are mowing the lawn, driving to work, watching TV, spending time with our children, sitting on the toilet, or doing the dishes, God is all around us, loving us as His precious children.

The gospel of the Happy Trinity has implications for our lives. From drinking in the love of Christ, to having supernatural ecstasies like the apostles, to being aware of God's presence in our day to day lives, there is joy available for today. This gospel is more than just a nice teaching— it's something real that can give us a fulfilling and abundant life. Enjoy a drink today!

---

57. Lawrence, The Practice of the Presence of God, 37.

Chapter Nine: The Apocalypse of the Happy Trinity

> *"And He who was seated on the throne said, 'Behold, I am making all things new.'"*
> Revelation 21:5

Let's talk about the "end-times."

This is a topic that is usually either loved or completely avoided out of fear. Yet it's really important to look at it, because how we view the end of the world affects how we live in the present. If we are all just going to die and then live as angels in the sky, that's not a lot of motivation for our present lives. If the world if just going to burn up in flames one day, then what does life matter?

As a matter of fact, the term "end-times" is only half the picture. Yes, evil and bad things are "ending," but that means that glorious things are "beginning." So, when you think of the "end-times" you should also think "new-beginning-times." It will be the end of all sadness, crying, and pain. "He will wipe away every tear from their eyes, and death shall be no more, neither shall there be mourning, nor crying, nor pain anymore, for the former things have passed away" (Revelation 21:4). The end-times will be the beginning of joyful times for planet earth.

Can you imagine the infinitely happy Father God of the universe personally wiping away people's tears for good? Why are we afraid of the future? We have nothing but good things coming our way!

Paul describes *God's will* as God's *good pleasure*. He wrote to the Ephesians that it is the "good pleasure of God's will" to bring *everything in heaven and on earth* into unity under Christ (Ephesians 1:9-10 KJV). When it comes to the future, we can rest assured that God's joyful pleasure is leading the entire universe into the love of Christ.[58]

We can trust our Dad.

The Apocalypse

First, let's look at the word "apocalypse." Usually when people hear this word their minds are flooded with images of fire-breathing demons, cities burning and collapsing, and scenes from cheesy Christian movies about the future. Oh, how the devil has tricked us on this one!

The word "apocalypse" comes from the Bible. It's in the very first sentence of the book of Revelation. The word comes from the Greek word *apokalypsis* and it

---

58. As stated earlier in the "Wrath of the Trinity" chapter, there will always be a place of "wrath" for those who reject the gospel.

CHAPTER NINE: THE APOCALYPSE OF THE HAPPY TRINITY

simply means "revelation."[59] It's a word that's used when something is hidden, but then comes out into the open. Paul used this word when he prayed to the Father and asked that we would have the Spirit of wisdom and *apokalypsis* (Ephesians 1:17).

In reality, the apocalypse is simply about God being revealed. Right now, everything is hidden. Jesus is not physically here so everything must be taken *by faith*. The Father, the Son, and the Spirit are all hiding throughout the world. However, the apocalypse is coming and one day God will be revealed for the whole world to see!

We have been raised with Christ and are currently seated with Him in heavenly places (Colossians 3:1). We can experience it by faith, but it's still hidden to the world and only those with eyes of faith can see it. Paul said, "Your life is hidden with Christ in God. When Christ who is your life is *revealed*, then you also will be *revealed* with Him in glory" (Colossians 3:3-4 NASB). While the events of the "apocalypse" might entail many things, we cannot lose sight of the fact that it is ultimately about the glorious revealing of Jesus for the whole world to see.

The Last Days

Now let's talk briefly about the commonly used phrase, "the end-times." If you're a Christian (and even if you're not), you've most likely heard people talk about this subject. Once again, this phrase usually fills people's

---

59. "Lexicon: Strong's G602: Apokalypsis" (https://www.blueletterbible.org/lang/lexicon/lexicon.cfm?Strongs=G602&t=KJV).

minds with image such as earthquakes, tsunamis, wars, and many other tragedies. But let's talk about the Biblical meaning of this phrase.

The concept of the end-times can be traced back to the prophecies of the Old Testament. The Hebrew prophets told of the "last days" when God would intervene in the world and do a new thing. The Jews saw the "last days," or "end-times," as a wonderfully good thing. They understood it as a time when God's Messiah would restore the world and fulfill all the promises of God. These promises included things like world peace, financial prosperity, abundant joy, peace with the animals, and the outpouring of the Holy Spirit.

One important example of these prophecies comes from the second chapter of the book of Joel. Joel prophesied, "In the *last days* it will be, God declares, that I will pour out My Spirit upon all flesh, and your sons and your daughters shall prophesy" (Joel 2:28). In the book of Acts, the apostle Peter quoted this prophecy and he actually declared that the "last days" were *at hand*. He announced that the promised Spirit who was to be poured out in the last days was being poured out before the people's eyes through Jesus the Messiah. (see Acts 2:17-36)

We have been living in the "last days" or the "end-times" since Jesus rose from the dead. His resurrection marked a new stage in history. At that point, we entered into the time where Jesus was seated at the right hand of God and the promised Spirit was being poured out on all flesh. To this day, we are still in this stage in history. Jesus

CHAPTER NINE: THE APOCALYPSE OF THE HAPPY TRINITY

is still seated on the throne and He is still pouring out His Spirit on all flesh. We are now living in the last days and rejoicing in the Lord, while also waiting for the glorious apocalypse (revealing) of all that is hidden.

"I the Lord Do Not Change"

So, what exactly is going to be revealed at the apocalypse? Well, if you've been reading up to this point you can already guess. If you're hoping that God changes from a Happy Trinity to some other God, then you will be sorely disappointed. God does not change. "Jesus Christ is the same yesterday and today and forever" (Hebrews 13:8).

The same Jesus who loved the world and laid down His life for the world is going to be revealed to the entire world. The Father who delights in us and parties with music and dancing is going to be clearly seen by everyone. You see, God really does not change. When the Psalmist said, "His mercy endures forever," he meant it (Psalm 136). God's joyful mercy toward us will never waver and, in fact, it will last forever—and ever.

Jesus taught His disciples that they would one day be rewarded for merely giving a glass of water to someone (Matthew 10:42)! That's the kind of King we are dealing with at the apocalypse. The Messiah who is going to be revealed has the heart to reward people for *merely giving away a glass of water.* How many more millions of things will we be rewarded for? Remember when you shared your Cheetos with your friend? Jesus remembers and He will reward you for that. Or what about when you picked up your wife's socks off the ground for her. *Another reward from Jesus.* Or the time you let that lady in the minivan make the left-hand turn before you? *More rewards.* It's going to be an over-the-top celebration filled with heavenly generosity. If God gave His one and only Son for us, how much more will He give at the glorious day of His revealing?

There is a day coming when the God who loves the whole world with an unfailing love will reveal Himself in all of His glory. Far from being a day that we should fear, this is going to be one of the greatest days in all of human history. The apostle John literally told us to have *boldness* and *no fear* on the day of judgment, because God is love (1 John 4:16-18).

The Day of Judgment

And yet there is a day of judgment coming. But if John tells us to have boldness and to not be afraid on this day, then what is this day all about? I think Jesus's parable of the prodigal son paints a great picture of this day and puts it in a powerful context.

In this famous parable, the prodigal son comes home and his father hugs and kisses him. He then gives him a robe and a ring and throws him a wild party with a fattened calf, wine, music, and dancing. In the story, the prodigal's older brother gets jealous and refuses to join the party. The father then goes outside and talks to him, but the older brother is bitter about the party. The father corrects him and tells him, "I am with you always and all that is mine is yours" (Luke 15:31).

CHAPTER NINE: THE APOCALYPSE OF THE HAPPY TRINITY

Herein lies the day of judgment. All of creation was created to be a joyful party. The Happy Trinity created this planet to be a celebration of God's Goodness. The world is destined to be a party forever in the love of the Father, Son, and Spirit! But there is a judgment coming that will manifest against every "older brother" who remains bitterly offended and *refuses to enter the Father's party.*

This is seen clearly in Zechariah 14. Zechariah prophesied of the time when God would be revealed to all the nations. He went on to say that "all the nations" will go up to worship the King and "to celebrate the Feast of Tabernacles" (Zechariah 14:16). The Feast of Tabernacles was a week-long celebration for the people of God. They would all set up tents and eat and drink and be merry in God's holy presence.

Zechariah said that whoever did not come and celebrate would be judged through the withholding of rain. You can see here the same kind of judgment as in the parable of the prodigal son. The Father *desires* to have a celebration with all nations. Yet, whoever refuses to celebrate stands judged. They remain outside the celebration and thus cannot take part in any of its benefits and blessings. It's ironic that it's ultimately God's *goodness* that carries a "judgment" toward anyone who refuses that goodness!

On the day of judgment, God's great party is going to be revealed in all its splendor, power, and love. The judgment will be upon those who reject His free gift of forgiveness and love. This will simply be the open manifestation of what already happens in a hidden way now. For those who believe, there is a party of joy and love in this life, even now. Anybody can receive this free gift by faith. Unfortunately, many people reject it, because it all just seems so foolish.

Tremble at His Goodness

There's another wonderful prophecy that describes the apocalypse and it's found in the book of Hosea. It says that the people "will come trembling to the Lord *and to His goodness* in the last days" (Hosea 3:5 NASB). This is a great picture of what that day will look like. Will there be fear and trembling? You betcha! The living God who has the power to create and hold together millions of galaxies is going to be revealed in all His goodness!

Isaiah also prophesied, "And the glory of the Lord shall be revealed, and all flesh shall see it together, for the mouth of the Lord has spoken" (Isaiah 40:5). The whole world is going to tremble at the goodness and glory of God!

Now to bring the prophecies of Hosea and Isaiah together—Moses helped us see that God's glory *is His goodness* (Exodus 33:18-19). And so the whole world will be completely stunned at the smiling goodness of God! Zephaniah prophesied that the Lord would rejoice over us with singing (Zephaniah 3:17). Can you imagine the living God visibly and audibly singing over billions of people from every nation with joyful songs?

There will be an incredible "awe factor" to all of this. We are not dealing with a "joy" that is weak and passive. The God of the universe is going to *make Himself known*

CHAPTER NINE: THE APOCALYPSE OF THE HAPPY TRINITY

to every person, city, and nation. It's going to be the most wonderful thing to witness. Our heavenly Dad and our Big Brother Jesus are going to put on quite a show!

We will be ready with open hearts for whatever He wants to do! We trust Him! He has been our loving Savior all along and He has promised not to change! If anybody gives Him a hard time they will end up having a hard time themselves. But it is completely our Papa's desire for all people to receive His goodness (1 Timothy 2:4).

The Lamb Makes All Things New

We have a glorious future ahead of us. Jesus said, "The meek will inherit the earth" (Matthew 5:5). God created this world in the beginning and said it was "very good." And now, His plan is to destroy all the corruptive and destructive systems of mankind. This is a huge part of what the Bible means when it says God is making *all things new*.

God is going to restore the world and make it beautiful. Habakkuk prophesied that the whole earth will be filled with the *knowledge* of the glory of the Lord (Habakkuk 2:14). The key in understanding this verse is to realize that the whole earth is *already* full of His glory (Isaiah 6:3). One day, the whole earth shall *know it*. And how is this all going to happen?

The Lamb is making it happen.

The "Lamb" is the image that the book of Revelation uses to describe Jesus. The devil has purposely lied so much about the book of Revelation, because he is so afraid of it. How funny is it that we have been so afraid of a book with a *Lamb* as its leading character! The first Christians were incredibly comforted by the book of Revelation, for they realized that the Lamb who loved them and died for them was the One in charge of the world.

This is the great promise and hope of the book of Revelation—God the Father, His Son the Lamb, and the wild and free Holy Spirit are making all things new (Revelation 21:5). No matter what the news, false prophets, fearful pastors, and your worried grandma says, this *world is headed for glory.* Jesus, the Lamb of the world, who died to heal it, is working throughout all of history to make everything right again. All the pain, all the tears, and all the struggles of humanity are going to be healed and personally taken care of by Jesus.

The promise of the Good News is that we are all going to live forever. Even though we might die or get martyred, we will come back to life. "Do not be astonished at this; for the hour is coming when all who are in their graves will hear His voice and will come out," Jesus said (John 5:28-29). We get to live forever! We will be reunited with friends and family and many people throughout history. We will witness reconciliation between people who killed each other in the previous life! We will all celebrate with our heavenly Father and our Savior Jesus.

Nations will no longer wage war against each other as world leaders learn to love just as they are loved by God (Isaiah 2:4). There will be a sharing of food, money, and resources like never before seen in the history of the

CHAPTER NINE: THE APOCALYPSE OF THE HAPPY TRINITY

world. The sons and daughters of God will reach levels of creativity that we can't even dream about yet. The earth is groaning for the sons and daughters to be revealed with Jesus (Romans 8:19). All the nations will rejoice and be glad, because they will discover how amazing God is (Psalm 67:4)! And in all of this, even throughout eternity, we will praise the Father, Son, and Holy Spirit.

Epilogue: How Then, Shall We Live?

"The joy of the Lord is your strength."
Nehemiah 8:10

If God is a Happy Trinity; if He has accomplished salvation through the death and resurrection of Christ, and is going to make all things new—*how then, shall we live?*

There's an amazing story in the Old Testament that gives us a little bit of insight here. Abraham, the forefather of our faith, was hanging out by his tent one day when three visitors show up. He immediately recognizes something special about them and welcomes them into his home. He serves them and washes their feet while his wife Sarah cooks up some pancakes for them to enjoy. Soon enough, Abraham realizes he's in the presence of God Himself—in three different Persons (Genesis 18:31-15).

After a simple time of food and relaxation, the Three give Abraham amazingly good news. They tell him his wife is going to miraculously give birth to a child within a year.

THE HAPPY TRINITY

Sarah, who is way past the age of childbearing, overhears the conversation and laughs to herself. This laughter is what leads to the name of the child. The following year, Sarah gives birth and is filled with joy. They decide to name the baby "Isaac," which literally means *laughter* (Genesis 21:5-6).

In the same way, we are called to hang out with the Happy Trinity and get to know Them and receive Their wonderful "good news!" Out of this, we are supernaturally impregnated with Their very nature! Just like Sarah, we too give birth to the laughter of God! In fact, the apostle Paul tells us that we are like the children of Sarah and are called to follow her example. This is where we learn about the fruit of the Holy Spirit (Galatians 5:22).

And that is our calling. To *walk in the Spirit* of our gracious Father and our Big Brother Jesus. This Spirit, in whom we are called to walk, is One of love, joy, peace, patience, kindness, goodness, faithfulness, gentleness, and self-control. These are the *fruits* that are to fill our new way of life.

> *"But the fruit of the Spirit is love, joy, peace, patience, kindness, goodness, faithfulness, gentleness, self-control; against such things there is no law."*
> (Galatians 5:22-23)

The Song of Songs gives us a beautiful picture of how God relates to these *fruits* within us. In the Song, the Bride says to her Beloved, "Let my beloved come to his garden,

EPILOGUE: HOW THEN, SHALL WE LIVE?

and eat its choicest fruits" (Song of Songs 4:16). We are like the Bride, asking God to eat the fruit of the Spirit within us.

The Beloved, who symbolizes God, responds and says, "I came to my garden, my sister, my bride, I gathered my myrrh with my spice, I ate my honeycomb with my honey, I drank my wine with my milk" (Song of Songs 5:1). Amazingly, God enjoys the fruit that the Spirit bears within us! God adds, "Eat, friends, drink, and be drunk with love!"

Watchman Nee, a 20th century church leader and teacher in China who was persecuted for his faith to the point of dying for Christ in prison, wrote the following commentary on this verse: "The Beloved answers, inviting His beloved 'friends,' the Triune God, to eat, drink, and drink deeply, to enjoy her with Him."[60]

The Trinity drinks and eats the fruit of our lives. It is *intoxicating* to Him. The Father drinks of the Son within us. And the Son drinks of the Father within us. And They both drink of the Spirit who is within us! It's a love feast!

The Fruit of the Spirit

We are to live in love, because God first loved us. Since God perfectly loves us, we are to love others. Jesus displayed the fullness of His love for us on the cross. We know that nothing can ever separate us from this love. It

---
60. Watchman Nee, *Song of Songs,* (Christian Literature Crusade, 1966), 34.

is our assurance in this love that frees us to love others without pressure.

We live in joy, because we are so safe in our Dad's loving arms. We have joy because His joy is in us. We smile, because we feel His smile over us. We are happy, because all of our sins are forgiven, and we can rest in what He accomplished on the cross.

We live in peace, because we have ceased from our labors and entered into the rest of His finished work. We have already been raised and seated into the highest throne of heaven, the very throne of Christ! We can relax, because He did the work for us to receive every blessing of heaven and all the fullness of God (Ephesians 1:3 & 2:6).

In this great victory, Christ has disarmed all the principalities and demonic powers of the universe (Colossians 2:15). We have peace now because we trust that our happy Father is working out all things for our good (Romans 8:28). No matter how the world looks, we trust that the Lamb has taken away the sins of the world (John 1:29). We know that the Happy Trinity is restoring everything and that the whole earth will be filled with the knowledge of the glory of the Lord! (Habakkuk 2:4)

We have patience, because we know how unbelievably patient our happy Father is. We are in no rush, because we sense that the Holy Spirit isn't either. Jesus is completely at rest in the love of His Father and so are we.

EPILOGUE: HOW THEN, SHALL WE LIVE?

We are kind and good, because joyful Jesus is always kind and good to us. His grace comes from the abundant joy that He receives from His Father. We are kind, because God has dealt kindly with us, not counting our sins against us. We are good to people, because God has been so good to us, stooping into our lives and loving our weak hearts.

We are faithful, because we have no one else to turn to. If we are not faithful to our Happy God, we will be faithful to other idols. We will turn to lesser gods, which are really no gods at all. We will settle for lesser pleasures, which are really no pleasures at all. And even when we don't "feel" God's presence, we are faithful because of what He did on the cross. It is a true and lasting work whether or not we feel it (or understand it).

We are gentle, because our heavenly Father is our big, friendly giant. He has called us friends. He has gently lifted up His little children into heavenly places. He kneels down and washes our feet. He is lowly and humble of heart and as we see this side of Him, we naturally become gentle toward others.

We have self-control, because we trust our Holy Savior and understand that He gives us boundaries to keep us in the most happiness possible. We control ourselves from all manner of evil and abide in His pure joy and perfect love. We enjoy a sound mind in the presence of the Happy Trinity, the fullness of joy.

The fruit of the Spirit flows into our relationships with others. Therefore, husbands, love your wives. Love yourselves as much as God does and you will be so filled

THE HAPPY TRINITY

with joy that humility will become your nature. Have fun with your wives and be playful with them. Do things that they like. Don't take yourself too seriously, but be the light of your family.

Wives, celebrate your husbands. Help them always; they need it! Know that you are a wife to Jesus before you are a wife to your husband. Let Christ be affectionate with you. Then, enjoy all the blessings that you and your husband are receiving from your heavenly Dad.

Have fun with your kids, because this pleases the God who has fun in heaven every day. Also, teach your kids difficult things about life so they are prepared when they grow up. Be stern with them at times, but always return to that place of joyful love.

Children, respect your parents and listen to them. They know better than you. If you do what they say, you will be very happy for the rest of your life. Jesus is your best friend forever and He plays with you every day. Pray to Him all the time about everything.

All of you who work a day job, shine your light. Be ready with a creative word from God when the time is right. Be a beacon of consistency, joy, love, and peace. Don't just go along with anything and everything but stand up for what is right.

Love the poor, the widows, the orphans, and all of those who are hurting. Jesus taught that whatever you do for people in need, you are doing for Jesus Himself (Matthew 25). "See" Jesus in the worst of the worst and let love break

EPILOGUE: HOW THEN, SHALL WE LIVE?

through. Go out and find the enemies, find the broken, find the needy, and show them the Father's love. He wants them to come home as well. When you suffer persecution for your love of Jesus, know that you are blessed beyond measure. Even if you are killed for your faith, you will rule as a king and priest in the age to come.

Welcome Home

This has been a wonderful journey. We have now arrived at our home in the Happy Trinity. As we come to the end of our journey, listen to one last story from the Son as He describes your homecoming to the Father.

> *"So he returned home to his father. And while he was still a long distance away, his father saw him coming, and was filled with loving pity and ran and embraced him and kissed him.*
>
> *His son said to him, 'Father, I have sinned against heaven and you, and am not worthy of being called your son—'*
>
> *But his father said to the slaves, 'Quick! Bring the finest robe in the house and put it on him. And a jeweled ring for his finger; and shoes! And kill the calf we have in the fattening pen.*

THE HAPPY TRINITY

We must celebrate with a feast, for this son of mine was dead and has returned to life. He was lost and is found.'

So the party began."
(Luke 15:20-24 TLB)

Find out more at
www.TheHappyTrinity.com

Follow Dylan and his wife Whitney's missionary journey at
www.theDemarsicos.com

Dylan DeMarsico is also the co-founder of Elisha's Riddle — an online magazine that unfolds the glorious mysteries of God. Every subscription supports a happy, trinitarian model of addiction recovery.

Discover more at
www.ElishasRiddle.com

More Books from Eyes Open Press

The Song of the Ages Series
By Nick Padovani

Go deeper into the heart of God and the wondrous mysteries of who we are in Him. Follow in the footsteps of the Shulammite in the Song of Songs and discover the limitless treasures of our union with Christ. A wonderful companion to The Happy Trinity.

And coming soon: *Part III: Eden's Return*

Available at Amazon and www.NickPadovani.com

www.ingramcontent.com/pod-product-compliance
Lightning Source LLC
Chambersburg PA
CBHW070433010526
44118CB00014B/2023